LEFT-RIGHT

The March of Political Extremism in Britain

A Platform Book

LEFT-RIGHT

*The March of Political
Extremism in Britain*

by

John Tomlinson

John Calder · London
Riverrun · New York

First published in Great Britain 1981 by
John Calder (Publishers) Ltd
18 Brewer Street, London W1R 4AS
and in the U.S.A. 1981 by
Riverrun Press Inc.
Suite 814, 175 Fifth Avenue, New York 10010

BRITISH LIBRARY CATALOGUING IN PUBLICATION DATA
Tomlinson, John
    Left right. – (Platform)
    1. Political parties – Great Britain
    2. Right and left (Political science)
    I. Title   II. Series
    322.4'2'0941   JN1121

    ISBN 0 7145 3855 8 paper bound

Photoset in 11 point Times by
Specialised Offset Services Limited, Liverpool
Printed and Bound in the U.K.
by Mansell (Bookbinders) Ltd., Witham, Essex

ERRATUM

On page 51 in line 5 it is said that Martin Wingfield, a National Front organiser, was convicted in 1979 for an assault upon a Jewish café owner. The author and publishers admit this is a mistake and apologise for the error. It was Raymond Hill mentioned in line 4 who was so convicted. Mr Wingfield has never been convicted of any such assault.

Contents

List of Illustrations

Diagrams

LORD HANKEY: My Lords, before we leave this matter, may I ask the noble Lord to enlighten us as to what is the League of St George? Is it Left wing or Right wing, and why is it interested in making bombs?

LORD BELSTEAD: My Lords, I think that both the noble Lord, Lord Brockway, and I would agree that it is just plain subversive.

LORD ELWYN-JONES: A good adjective, my Lords.

Wednesday, 26 November 1980
HANSARD

Foreword

This is a timely book.

Extremist groups are becoming endemic in Britain, a threat to the country and the allies, conscious or unconscious, of terrorism. Terrorism, as Mr Tomlinson points out, is now an international network, amply supplied with funds and operating in many countries.

The book deals with the general background, beliefs and philosophy (if any) of extremist groups. It then gives a detailed description of particular groups.

The reader may be puzzled on two counts. He or she may feel that undue importance is given to some groups: it may be felt that the author's assessment of some of their activities is wrong. This is inevitable. As the author points out, he is exploring territory not only largely unknown but which wishes to remain unknown. Further, personal judgement is bound to play a part in any assessment of the activities discussed. I have my own reservations. But as not only a democrat but as someone who believes in the presuppositions upon which democracy must be founded I find this book well informed and its conclusions in general sound and certainly apposite.

The other cause of puzzlement may be the great number of left-wing socialist groups, many with similar names, splitting, waxing, waning, amalgamating. The reader may well become confused. But it is valuable to have a dictionary, so to speak, to which one can refer.

It is interesting to read of the small membership of extremist groups but we should not be misled by the figures. Such groups are not negligible because they are small. In every country which they have taken over from 1917 onwards the Communists have been a tiny minority. The technique of the most dangerous groups, the factions on the extreme left, is to infiltrate existing organisations, in particular the Labour Party and the Trades Unions. Terrorist groups are even smaller. But by their determination to use violence of every sort they can subvert free government, force their opponents into retaliation and thereby hope to create a situation favourable to revolution and dictatorship.

Further, though the groups may be small, the powers behind them are not. Nor are the methods used unsophisticated. Some of the most fascinating parts of the book lift the curtain behind which such groups would like to hide, and reveal the variety of their methods. Read this account of the PLO:

> In essence the 'two-track' strategy is extremely simple; while the PLO strives energetically to build upon its reputation as a political and diplomatic mission, it deputes its less 'moderate', and consequently more embarrassing, activities to other extremist groups on its payroll. The fact that the PLO clients themselves have no more in common with each other besides their extremism only serves to emphasise the point that terrorism has become a kind of multi-national industry devoid entirely of any ideological idealism or piety – a factor which makes it all the more difficult to predict or anticipate.
>
> The direct consequences are threefold: firstly, the PLO achieves its terrorist ends, and without undue publicity; secondly, extremist groups gain otherwise unexpected funds, experience, weaponry and contacts; thirdly, those influences which guide the PLO fulfil their own objectives.
>
> For not even the PLO is prime-mover in the terrorist international. Without the financial subsidy of Syria, Libya, Iraq, and Saudi Arabia, without the support of Cuba, Algeria and Vietnam, and most significant in this context, without the tutelage and patronage of the Soviet Union, the PLO itself would be no more than a small and savage band of guerillas.

Terrorist groups are already supplied with modern weapons, through the USSR, Cuba or various Middle Eastern or East European states and factions: there is no reason why they should not be given nuclear weapons. So far no weapon found in the possession of the murderers of the Red Brigades in Italy has been made in that country.

None of this is entirely new. We are all vaguely aware of the assassinations and kidnappings, the sophisticated weapons of the IRA, the attacks by Cubans. But there is still a feeling of complacency. Isn't it partly the usual sensationalism of the Press? Won't it defeat itself? Surely someone (not we ourselves) will do something about it? Won't it just go away? Here is evidence that it will not go away. Too many people and too many rich and powerful people don't want it to go away.

At present in this country it is not so much terrorism as infiltrations such as that of the Labour Party by the Militant Tendency which cause alarm, despite Northern Ireland and the Iranian Embassy. It is at the moment causing more alarm than those groups which do not practice 'entrism' as it is called. For dangerous though these may become by attacking the police, fomenting strikes, inciting demonstrations, they are identifiable. But those who join parties to subvert them from within work like dry rot – their labours may not affect the look of the fabric until it collapses.

It is difficult enough for the liberals (of all parties) to respond to the revolutionaries outside their parties, without damaging the very tolerance by which liberalism survives. It is even more difficult when such wreckers join the parties under the guise of good democrats. This technique is well-known. They succeed by perseverance and the infliction of boredom on their opponents. But democrats are rightly chary of cutting short debate. As the author says, the political parties should at least be aware of what is happening. It is up to them to take appropriate measures. There are of course border-line cases, but there is not really much difficulty in distinguishing between the Monday Club and the National Front, or some followers of Tony Benn and the Communists. It is probably in the Trades Unions that the difficulties and dangers are most acute.

At the end of this book the author gives five recommendations. I would add three more. First, I am not so sceptical about legal action as is the author. I agree that legal action cannot take the place of vigilance by us all. But I do believe that some changes in the law are necessary to limit the opportunities for our enemies to make trouble. Secondly, I am sure that children are not sufficiently educated in the presuppositions of a free society. Indeed, many teachers reject such a society. Education is a vital field. Thirdly, we are being indoctrinated with the view that we have little individual responsibility: decisions must be left to bureaucratic organisations: we must simply obey. I am horrified by the ease with which minorities get their way. People all too easily surrender and acquiesce in what they know is wrong. Nor will they 'interfere'. All too often they ignore even muggings in the streets. They too seldom report criminals or criminal activities of which they must be aware. And the police have largely lost their local contacts. This makes an ideal atmosphere in which militants can swim and intimidate.

A valuable book – I hope that not only those interested in politics but all those who want a decent, free, democratic Britain will take it to heart.

J. GRIMOND

LEFT-RIGHT

The March of Political Extremism in Britain

Preface

The report which follows is the result of considerable research into the composition, activities, ambitions and strategies of Britain's extremist political groups. It is neither comprehensive in scope, nor necessarily complete in detail. But it is designed to serve as basic introduction to the sinister underworld of domestic politics. Some of the groups examined engage quite incontrovertibly in illegal and illegitimate activities. Others, for instance the Communist Party of Great Britain, offend only in spirit. The reader will no doubt exercise his own judgement and form his own conclusions.

The purpose of the paper is to inform, not to proselytise any particular or partial political point of view. The parties of the left and right often are possessed of their own distinctive 'house-style'; none is preferred although some are clearly more offensive or more menacing than others. It is hoped that this paper will fill a vacuum in what is undoubtedly a crucial area of national interest. But it is intended only as a discussion document, as impartial as may be possible, and as a form of encouragement and incentive to those better qualified and more authoritative to make the investigations and take the initiatives which this research has revealed to be both appropriate and necessary.

The Democratic Society and the Problem of Extreme Politics

Over the last fifteen years, and particularly in the past decade, the democratic societies of Europe and North America have been made aware of forces at work within their own social fabric, even within their most important institutions, whose interests and influence cannot be deemed compatible with those of the majority – the 'silent majority' as it once was so aptly described. Yet democracy's response has not stemmed the steady and gradual advances which have lately been made by extremists of both right and left.

There are of course cogent, indeed vital, arguments which are periodically advanced which dismiss the threat of political extremism as a mere sociological phenomenon, or as a paranoid fantasy of one main political party or another. There are strong and crucial arguments which warn of the consequences to liberal democracy through institutional over-reaction to what are after all numerically inconsiderable extremist factions.

The purpose of this report however, is to point out to the public that many of these factions have no regard whatsoever for the liberal niceties of democratic tolerance and accommodation, that they indeed respect them only in so far as they offer protection and the opportunity for the advancement of inimical causes, and that these factions have achieved a capacity for subversion and disruption which far surpasses their strength of numbers. In view of our present perilous economic position and the various predictions for the decade which prophesy recession, slump and all the concommittant economic and social strains on which the extremist groups depend for the stimulation of their membership and influence, and from which they have profitted in recent years, this report is intended as a timely and critical analysis of the interests, organisation and activities of some of the more significant extremist groups which would otherwise prefer to control their own publicity.

Extremism in Theory

Allusion has been made to those arguments which, for the sake of democracy, counsel against over-reaction to political extremism. Clearly it would be dramatic but unconstructive to overestimate the influence and capacity of the extremists. On the other hand, this report precedes from the premis that democracy should 'know its enemy', and from the conviction that heretofore the activity of extremists has been seriously underestimated and unremarked. This point has only very recently been exemplified by what may be ultimately the most significant feature of the 'Militant Affair': that despite the combined column footage of such serious publications as *The Times* and *Sunday Times,* the *Daily Telegraph* and *Sunday Telegraph*, the *Guardian* and the *Observer*, the *New Society* and the *New Statesman*, there have been *no substantive revelations* as to the nature and conduct of the 'Militant Tendency' which were not already known or available to an interested political observer. One may conclude that this lack of real disclosure signifies that the Tendency is in fact fundamentally innocuous. In a subsequent section, this paper will suggest otherwise; initially however, two important inferences may be drawn from this example:

1. That Militant's recent success has been largely derived from the low profile it has preserved.

2. That it is sufficiently well-equipped in terms of organisation and discipline to resist the investigative efforts of powerful and influential journals.

The fact that it has firmly established itself within the Labour Party is indisputable. However, the fact that the Militant Tendency has become a *cause célèbre* should serve to underline the suggestion that that faction is only one of many cells, groups and organisations which quietly contest the nether regions of political influence.

Proceeding from the principle of 'know thy enemy', the first and paramount priority must be to establish criteria by which to identify that enemy. This is not a simple task, as the debate within the Labour Party over Militant activities has recently illustrated.

Democracy must necessarily remain a 'broad church', not only in order to preserve its fundamental freedoms, but also in order to sustain the political and intellectual dialogue on which its vitality depends. It is therefore crucial at the outset to recognise the distinction between 'radicality' and 'extremism'.

The radical critique, whether emanating from the Conservative Monday Club, the Labour Tribune Group or from one or other interest group, is one which seeks to challenge the balance of elements within the existing socio-economic status quo. It accepts implicitly the principle of liberal democracy and its motive, while ranging from the reactionary to the reformist, corresponds to that principle. To this extent, radical opinion of both left and right, in recognising and sharing the concept and institution of democracy as 'ideal', is in that regard conservative or rather, preservative. Its prescriptions are constructive and remedial and in accord with democratic method; while one may not subscribe to the particular radical position, one would not wish to challenge it except through the force of counter argument and mandate.

The extremist critique is however profoundly different. While it too makes appeal to the democratic motive, its interpretation and enactment of that principle is essentially 'anti-social'. It advances a critique of society which is fundamental; not reformist – an instinct which is anathema to the extremist – but revolutionary. It expresses a view not compatible with that of any majority and promotes it in a manner often at best extra-democratic and at worst anti-democratic.

In short, the extremist subscribes to and promotes a social critique the end of which, and often the means also, is implicitly anti-democratic within the understanding of the liberal tradition and its prevailing institutions.

Extremism in Practice

None of the extremist groups seriously imagine that the overthrow of British liberal democracy is an immediate possibility, though their prophesies are dire. On the left particularly, extremists have learnt from past experience that Capital is more resilient than dialectical materialism had led them to believe. The classic extremist strategy is therefore parasitic, exploitative and provocative.

Excluding principally the National Front and the Workers' Revolutionary Party, extremist groups have spurned the electoral process; not only are they aware that the polls will afford them no kind of success, but also for ideological and tactical reasons they have sought to build their political power bases more subtly. On the left some factions have sought shelter within the legitimacy of the Labour Party where through both application and intrigue they have acquired substantial influence and authority, as they have also within the Trades Union movement. On the right the Conservative Monday Club has been a target for infiltration as have the various rightist pressure groups. In both cases extremists can be attributed at least in part with the hardening and polarisation of the programmes and attitudes of the major parties: Labour has effectively enhanced the prospects of the extreme left in order to appease the more moderate Tribune Group; the Conservatives have striven to steal National Front votes by stealing National Front thunder – Mrs Thatcher's pre-election speech on immigration being the prime example. In both cases, the main parties have been concerned to maintain control over their more radical wings, while at the same time blunting the challenge of the extremists. However, they may have established a precedent which the extremists will be grateful to exploit until the traditional political centre ground, the arena for debate and dialogue, becomes a vacuum in which the moderate voice is breathless. The accommodation of extremist views within the democratic institutions is not possible without the complete subversion of those institutions. This the extremists well know, especially the Trotskyists who believe that concerted and sustained pressure will ultimately compel liberal society to subvert itself in its efforts to avoid a more dramatic collapse.

The polarisation of political opinion is another condition by which extremists of both right and left believe, rightly, that they can profit. This has a three-fold appeal: firstly as suggested it denotes an accommodation of extreme positions; secondly, it imposes exploitable stress and conflict on society; thirdly, it provokes a response from government which ultimately serves to weaken the moderate cause. The result is a deteriorating syndrome.

If one can state that between the left and right radical formulations of criticism there is a common and central acceptance of democracy as 'ideal' and that dialogue and dispute flows legitimately and envigoratingly across that middle ground, this essential 'centralism' does not, by definition, apply to the left and right extremist groups. However, this 'communion of opposites' does find expression for the extremists, if not intellectually, then certainly in activity. In other words two distinct dangers arise:

firstly, neither extreme restrains the other through the moderation of discourse, and secondly, their particular communion finds expression in the form of mutual incitement, thus establishing an increasingly illegitimate and violent 'backlash' syndrome, common in theory only in that both reject democracy as the primary and central thesis, and in practice in that that rejection exemplifies their total lack of liberal inhibition in political activity. Faced with open warfare between the extremes, government is powerless; the rule of law cannot tolerate civil disorder, nor can it act to intervene without infringing basic liberal freedoms.

The most immediate example of this syndrome is not far from memory. The political right has first preyed upon the susceptibilities, prejudices and insecurity of potential recruits, then inflamed and exploited them, mobilising them into a racist campaign against immigration and immigrants. The immigrants, themselves disadvantaged, hard-pressed, threatened and insecure have in turn been enlisted and manipulated by the left and its allies in a crusade, ostensibly against fascism. Both factions situate and time their activities for maximum disturbance and publicity, converging simultaneously on the middle ground held by society's agents, the police. That centre ground is untenable; the police are accused by both right and left, and the police pressure government to introduce legislation whose implementation would have serious and unwelcome consequences for basic freedoms, again to be exploited by the extremist 'libertarians'.

Extremism: the Potential Threat

It is clear that both extremes have it in their interests to provoke or incite drastic social conflict or government intervention. It is clear also that they have not the slightest regard for democratic method or majority will in the pursuance of their own objectives, except when the dictates of pragmatic strategy demand lip-service. While it is true that Britain, with the exception of Northern Ireland, has not been visited with the level of political violence that has afflicted some of her neighbours, it is not unlikely that this is a prospect. Particularly on the right there exist fanatical well-equipped and trained cells, highly organised and secretive. Many of the left factions maintain contacts with international terrorist organisations, including the IRA and the PLO. Both right and left groups have foreign affiliations, some sustain foreign loyalties.

Liberalism with its crucial emphasis on freedom and tolerance is necessarily and unavoidably susceptible to extremist subversion and exploitation. Extreme measures, so gratifying to those at which they are aimed, will only be enacted when it is too late and the problem has become unmanageable. The task is rather to anticipate and to strengthen moderate resolve against extremist encroachment. To date the threat has not been regarded as sufficiently serious to stimulate the necessary attention and analysis; it has only been the symptom or by-product, violence, that has caught the eye. But it is a fact that extremists who are committed to an extra-parliamentary form of political activity, do not always ask to be taken seriously, sometimes indeed quite the opposite. It is, in this connection, salutary to note that as recently as March 1978, in an article entitled 'What future for the political fringe', the *Sunday Telegraph*, in stating that the Socialist Workers' Party was non-entrist, commented in brackets, '(another group, the "Militant Tendency", specialises in this)'; this was the only reference to the now (in)famous Tendency in a very long article. Militant was no doubt sufficiently gratified. There is more than anecdotal irony also in recalling the elation and sense of triumph many Americans experienced when, as they believed, their Constitutional system had been vindicated by the resignation of President Nixon. One need not acknowledge or accept that irony; however one cannot deny the bitterness and division which debilitated the nation and is active yet.

The argument of this paper then, is that the liberal society must fully appreciate its freedoms and commit itself to the principle and practice of its institutions if it is to protect them from subversion and render them inviolable against incursion. It must also identify and understand those groups and factions which intrigue and incite against it. When tolerance becomes complacency, it no longer is of any positive value. The threat is aptly illustrated in an extract from an interview with a former Militant member, printed in *New Society* of 10 January 1980. While reference is to Militant, it applies equally forcibly to any of the more serious groups of the far left or right:

> You'll never stop these people. They are working away all the time. They are all programmed to say the same things. They've got the knife into MPs, councillors and most of the NEC (Labour's National Executive Committee). People underestimate Militant. People think that if you don't worry about them, they will go away. But they're wrong.

The concern of this paper then, is to encourage awareness and discussion of those political attitudes which are incompatible with or counter to the interests of a free and liberal democracy, and to disclose as far as possible those extremist activities which are subversive and illegal, and actually and immediately prejudicial to the well-being of this country and all its citizens.

The Register of Extreme Parties

The previous section has with illustrations attempted to set out the range of objection to the principle and practice of extremist politics in a democratic society. These may be itemised in three distinct though related categories: Theory, Activity, Links. The organisations discussed in the following sections fall into one, two or all of these categories; in most cases this is beyond doubt; in some, however, lack of information or deliberate secrecy or ambivalence demands the qualified conviction of overwhelming circumstantial evidence; in a very few cases mention has been made of less disreputable groups whose contacts or infiltrated membership renders them vulnerable to serious subversion and arouses, albeit cautious, suspicion.

The criteria then are:

1. Theory
   a) That the ideology or objectives of such parties imply a *fundamental critique of society.*
   b) That the aims of these parties are *anti-democratic* and *anti-social.*

2. Activity
   a) That the activities of such parties are *covert* or *subversive.*
   b) That the strategies and activities of such parties are *illegal* or *criminal.*
   c) That the strategies of such parties involve the *use or potential of violence* and the *practice of discrimination.*

3. Links
   a) That such parties are *in receipt of covert and/or foreign funding.*
   b) That such parties are *allied or affiliated to, or represent the interests of individuals, groups or nations prejudicial to, or not compatible with the interests of liberal democracy.*
   c) That the aims and/or activities of these parties is *counter to the well-being and security of British democracy.*

The Right

Fascism, Nazism and the British Right

The 1960s marked a period of intense academic interest in the theory and practice of the politics of fascism. Yet in 1972, in surveying the accounts and explications which had resulted from so much research, H.A. Turner was obliged to comment (*World Politics* 24), that 'close to a decade of scholarly discussion has yielded nothing even approaching a consensus on the essential characteristics of fascism as a generic phenomenon, its causes, or even which movements and regimes properly deserve the title.'

Indeed, that many commentators feel that they may only responsibly refer to 'fascisms' well illustrates the difficulty which confronts those who strive to isolate the single and essential strain. To some extent, Joachim Fest's observation (*The Face of the Third Reich*) accounts for this central problem; in reviewing the nazi model he concluded that 'fundamentally National Socialism represented a politically organised contempt for the mind.' The apparent lack of coherent and rational ideological content in the fascist politic necessarily prohibits any definitive intellectual description. Fascism therefore, because it lacks its own generative stimulus, is seen as a largely reactive political expression dependent both for much of its form and its content upon the circumstance in which it arises. Because fascism can only be critically examined from a socio-psychological rather than from a socio-political point of view, since its political critique is essentially vacuous, analysts have been constrained to speak of Spanish fascism, German fascism, Italian fascism − in other words of 'fascisms' − and have failed to agree, as Turner noted, upon any universal fascist theory.

The 'contempt for the mind' to which Fest alludes, is primarily a condition of fascism's irrational ideology. But it extends further into the political mechanism of fascism. Indeed, as David Edgar points out (*Race and Class* 4), 'the very contradictions of the doctrine, and their irrational resolution, are at the core of its functional effectiveness as a mobilizer of support.' The appeal of fascism is to those sectors of capitalist society in crisis which feel most under social and economic threat and yet, while placing no faith in the ability of conventional or existing institutions to redress their disadvantages, similarly reject the revolutionary alternative of the left. The primary appeal therefore is to conservative elements of the economy seeking radical solution to a wide range of perceived ills. There can be no obvious intellectual or class basis for such a constituency; the appeal is to the disadvantaged – the excluded ruling class, the unprogressing lower middle class, the unorganised proletariat and the immobile peasantry. As David Edgar observes:

> The central problem of fascist ideology – the purpose of which is to mobilize the mass movement – is that the real interests of their various potential supporters are, in many cases, opposed.

As disparate as these potentially revolutionary elements are, their shared sense of alienation cannot as the unifying factor posit a shared future (as would the Marxist model) but rather regresses into a form of political, and almost necessarily partial and fantastical, nostalgia. The fascist critique is one which challenges capitalism not so much in theory as in practice. It rejects not private ownership, but multinationalism, speculative finance, economic internationalism. In other words it proscribes the advanced capitalism of the present, opposes a future-based Marxist model and embraces instead the past small, localised capitalism of personal ownership and self-dependence.

The distinction which both Mussolini and Hitler made between these alternative capitalisms was spuriously simplistic. Nevertheless it remains a tenet of the fascist economic thinking to distinguish between 'Good Capitalism' and 'Bad Capitalism' – the former being purely productive, the latter speculative and unearned. Ultimately, the distinction is between a national economy and an international economy.

But in fascist ideology, these distinctions are exemplary. The concept of self-maintenance and national priority extend from economic theory to political and social order. Internationalism, be it in finance or doctrine, is for the fascist inimical to the ordered and productive society. As Mussolini declaimed:

> Socialist theories have been disproved; internationalist myths have crumbled. The class struggle is a fairy tale, mankind cannot be divided.

Indeed for Mussolini, the corporate state was such an indivisible society, one in which 'everything (should be) inside the State, nothing outside the State, nothing against the State.' For the British fascist, the late Sir Oswald Mosley, the same emphatic priority applied. As Mosley wrote in *The Greater Britain*:

> There will be no room in Britain for those who do not accept the principle 'All for the State and the State for All.'

Clearly, there would be no room in such society for, for instance, a trade union movement – nor, for that matter, for an elected Opposition to Government. As Mosley rather elegantly put it in his 1938 publication *Tomorrow We Live*:

> In the light of history it will ever be regarded as a curious and temporary aberration of the human mind that great nations should elect a Government to do a job and should then elect an Opposition to stop them doing it.

The State entity is therefore the priority; national economy is in the classic model inimical to international finance, as is politically, national socialism to international socialism. But if Italian fascism was largely characterised by an aggressive opportunism and pragmatism, the nazi model sought the cohesion of disparate interests through a shared exclusivity, namely racism. The German nazis, in championing the indivisibility of the nation, could not seek to attain it by setting the oppressed proletariat against the industrialist, nor the petty bourgeois against the worker. Rather, the internationalism of business and the internationalism of the workers were conceived as the instruments of aliens who in effect comprised 'a state within the State'. While anti-Semitism and the conspiracy theory were by no means the invention of the nazis, they were perhaps their most notable contribution to the fascist ideology. As David Edgar points out:

> This theory posited a conscious, covert alliance between the international banker and monopolist on the one hand, and the international Marxist on the other. It sought, further, to racialise the plotters, so that the foe could be more readily differentiated from the friend.

It was a theory as potent in the 1930s for some British fascists as for the German NSDAP members. While Joseph Goebbels was claiming that 'it is because we want socialism that we are anti-Semitic' and while Hitler was supplying the complementary rhetoric that 'only an anti-Semite is a true anti-communist,' William Joyce

(*Fascism and Jewry*) asserted in 1936:

> The Jews control and activate alike the decadent democratic capitalism and the hideous fratricidal Communism. Using both instruments they hope to prevent every white people from achieving the freedom to work out the fullness of their own economic destiny. Only through the defeat of Jewry can Britain be free.

But moreover, it is theory still potent for and still characteristic of fascist groups in Britain. As the National Front 'Statement of Policy' had it:

> The National Front recognises that International Monopoly Capitalism is as great a menace to the freedom of the nations as International Communism, and that in fact the two represent different means to the same end: a world tyranny.

Nor is the National Front, and its right wing rivals and associates in Britain, in any doubt as to the perpetrators of this conspiracy. *The Protocols of the Elders of Zion* still serves as a bible for the anti-Semitic fascist and whilst its promoters may be obliged occasionally to disguise their references, the camouflage is thin. In 1976, the then editor of the National Front journal, Richard Verral, identified the enemy as:

> (1) International Finance, the parasite that feeds on nations and on free-enterprise industrial capitalism by the process of debt-creation, and which is predominantly Zionist in composition and Zionist in its global aims.
> (2) Marxism, a conspiracy fostered by the former.

It is crucial to recognise that for the National Front, the conspiracy theory is central to its world-view, such as it is. The notoriety which the Front has attracted for its attacks upon the black community in Britain is of course fully justified. But while racist propaganda asserts that the blacks are the ruination of the British nation both economically and racially, the same propaganda would portray the immigrants as the victims of multi-racialism, and the passive instruments of its promoters. Here again the parallel between nazi theory and that espoused by the National Front is quite clear. In *Mein Kampf*, Adolf Hitler wrote:

> It was and is the Jews who bring the negroes into the Rhineland, always with the same secret thought of their own of ruining the hated white race by the necessarily resulting bastardisation.

In October 1964, *Spearhead* proclaimed:

> If Britain were to become Jew-clean she would have no nigger neighbours to
> worry about.

The 'Jewish problem', of such pivotal importance to nazi fascism, is less overtly canvassed by British fascists. Nonetheless, it occupies a position central to the geometry of their irrational but, as David Edgar so correctly stresses, non-arbitrary ideological system.

Earlier, it was stated that there is no consensus as to the nature of fascism, only a series of descriptions of particular fascisms. The nazi model indeed, in its emphatic dependence upon nation and race and subsequently upon anti-Semitism was, though not of necessity, a contorted image of Italian fascism. In other words, German-type racism was to a large degree an adjunct to classic fascism, but one which the Italians could to some extent emulate. On the other hand, German theories of 'Aryanism' were exclusive of Italian imitation, necessarily.

Racism therefore, and particularly the Nordic variety, is a crucial touch-stone for those who wish to examine the correspondence between the nazi and non-nazi fascisms of the ignoble past on the one hand, and those which currently strive to flourish in Britain and elsewhere. For while, as the liberal consensus has it, fascism is of itself a manifest and gross evil, nazism, as the historical embodiment of fascism at its extreme, is the most obscene and grossest evil of all.

The Problem of 'Popular Usage'

It is a telling – and indeed disturbing – commentary on the current state of politics in Britain that the terminology of political positions has become the terminology of political abuse and it is significant to note that the bastardisation of political language has traditionally been the device of the extremists. Whereas in the past, the critique of liberalism remained the preserve of far left and far right, it is nowadays become almost fashionable to deride the centrist position as one connoting intellectual and political bankruptcy. Similarly, those to the left of centre are increasingly prepared to characterise the democratic right as 'fascist' and are in turn themselves rebuked as 'Marxists' or 'communists'.

In itself this trend may be distasteful, uncivilised, unintelligent. But it has also more serious consequences. First, because it provides for both the totalitarian left and right a propaganda screen behind which to mask, or even justify, their own respective excesses; secondly, and to a large degree in consequence, it induces in the public imagination so confused and generalised an understanding of extreme positions as to render it virtually insensible to real political villainy and incapable of distinguishing the fascist from the monetarist, the Marxist from the social democrat and indeed the nazi from the Trotskyite.

In the first case precedent is not difficult to locate. In cold war McCarthyite America the hint of the 'red under the bed', the application of the epithet 'commie' — or in fuller form, 'commie bastard' — irrespective of either justice or justification, could and frequently did destroy a career and a life. For a number of years, very few publically questioned the absurd and paradoxical concept of 'unamericanism', and still less challenged the motives, credentials or authority of Senator Joseph McCarthy. Indeed, long after McCarthy's fall from grace, many of his victims remain unrehabilitated and many of his chief aides have achieved high office, among them Richard Nixon and Robert Kennedy.

With somewhat more justification, but to a considerable extent for motives of its own, the far left Socialist Workers' Party in Britain has through its sponsorship of the Anti-Nazi League launched a recruitment drive avowedly against racism and fascism, but also by its own ideological implication, against state racism and state fascism, and ultimately against the state itself.

Indeed, the extreme right in Britain has at times sought to play both ends. In an article in the December 1974 issue of *Britain First*, at that time the National Front newspaper, it was blandly proposed that the anti-Tyndall faction of the Party was 'irrevocably committed to a belief in democratic nationalism, and reject(ed) all forms of authoritarianism.' The point is worthy of emphasis if only because those who cry loudest against the totalitarianism of the domestic communists and fascists and who take up the forward positions in the defence of liberal democracy — or who wish to reinforce it — are often those who do so expressly either to camouflage or to give free reign to their own impositions and excesses.

The second condition is both symptom and cause of a media-oriented society which contrives to by-pass the normal reasoning process of individual choice in favour of the quickly delivered and instantly recognisable 'tag' — a form of intellectual short-circuitry. Thus it is that while the anti-cults of Hitler and Stalin can be said to induce a horrible fascination in the imagination of the public, very little is understood of the ideologies which they espoused. Thus it is also, that when in July 1980, 600 British extremists of the right attended the annual Diksmuide nazi rally in Belgium, only one British national newspaper reported the event, and that paper was the *News of the World.*

But further, imprecise analysis and inexact or incautious use of language have profitted the extremists, and particularly those of the right. One glaring example of such critical imprecision has emanated from the United Nations itself. The authority which the UN has conferred upon ideological anti-Zionism has, amongst other things, effectively presented all anti-Semites with a cloak of respectability and legitimacy for their anti-Jewish propaganda. Not only may the anti-Semites pursue their objectives under the thin veil of anti-Zionism and thus escape the process of the Race Relations law in Britain, but also as a consequence of this authoritative 'loophole' and much to their delight, the alleged misdoings of the Zionists are increasingly to be found deposited upon the doorsteps of all Jews. The cynical manipulation of a legitimate objection to Zionism, coupled with public ignorance and institutional acquiescence, has made it ever more difficult, especially for Jewish communities throughout the world, to distinguish between anti-Zionism and anti-Semitism.

There is a further crucial problem in usage and understanding. The popular tendency of fusing the image of nazism with events rather than with the ideas and motives behind them has been increasingly exploited by the new nazis, who have come earnestly to believe that to free their ideology, without at all modifying it, from historical associations will ipso facto rehabilitate its political content. Accordingly the revisionist history which is currently pouring off right wing presses throughout the world – but especially in Britain, America, France and West Germany – argues with contrived academic authority that the mass murder of the Jews and others under the Third Reich simply did not occur. Every extreme right organisation advertises in its reading list the purified nazi legend propounded in such scholarship as *The Hoax of the Twentieth Century, Did Six Million Really Die?, The Myth of the Six Million* and many more similar in title and substance. Not only, they claim, is the Holocaust a massive fiction, but it is a fraud perpetrated upon the world by the purported victim, the Jew whose ruthless Zionism yet conspires to enslave mankind. Thus, with breathtaking succinctness, organised anti-Semitism strives simultaneously both to deny and to justify its racism and to promote the nazism of the future by vindicating the nazism of the past.

The debilitating danger of sloganised anti-fascism cannot be overstated, for it so devalues the cogent criticism against the real fascists, the real nazis, the real racists and their activities as severely to inhibit the fulfilment of the most basic necessity in political combat, that of identifying the enemy.

This volume does not claim to have established any definitive distinction between the various fascisms. By 'nazi' it is to be understood that the individual or group so described follows closely the fascism and anti-Semitism of the National Socialist Party (NSDAP) of the Third Reich. The application of the term 'fascist' refers to those individuals or groups which promote a fascist ideology not centrally dependent upon Aryan race theory and anti-Semitism.

The Register of the Right which follows attempts to identify that enemy in a recognisable and informed manner. The usage of the terms 'fascist' and 'nazi' has been applied where it is appropriate and has not been attributed gratuitously, arbitrarily or merely adjectively. The term 'neo-nazi' is redundant: either one is nazi or one is not.

Most of the extreme right groups in Britain, including the National Front, are nazi.

Perhaps no more than 20,000 people in Britain have committed their political allegiance to parties of the extreme right. Certainly, it is true to state that the radical right has never enjoyed in this country the intellectual and cultural tradition with which it has been associated particularly in the predominantly Catholic nations of Europe.

Many otherwise astute commentators of the political scene in Britain have on this basis been drawn to the bland assertion of what can be no more than a hopeful assumption, namely that Britons are as a people far too phlegmatic and altogether too pious to succumb to the dubious appeal of fascism. In some quarters, moreover, the eclipse of the National Front in the General Elections of May 1979 is assumed to have been total.

Against this background of political complacency, born of self-delusion and ignorance, it is indeed sadly ironic that this investigation, constituting the first comprehensive survey of political extremism in recent years, supplies evidence of a wide association

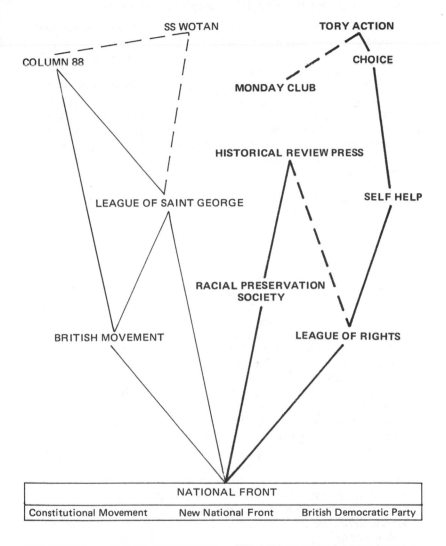

SS WOTAN

TORY ACTION

COLUMN 88

CHOICE

MONDAY CLUB

HISTORICAL REVIEW PRESS

LEAGUE OF SAINT GEORGE

SELF HELP

RACIAL PRESERVATION
SOCIETY

BRITISH MOVEMENT

LEAGUE OF RIGHTS

NATIONAL FRONT		
Constitutional Movement	New National Front	British Democratic Party

POLITICAL and PARA-MILITARY
GROUPS

PRESSURE AND PROPAGANDA
GROUPS

The National Front as front: the Extreme Right in Britain

and assortment of right-wing groups in Britain whose activities and resources are very much on the increase.

The possibility of a democratic espousal of fascism is not really at issue; disenchantment with mainstream politics is a serious but not immediately realisable threat on the broad scale. What is all too clear however, is that extremists do not need real political power or even reputation in order to make their unwelcome impact in society. It shall be shown that Martin Webster's promise that the National Front would 'kick its way into the headlines' is but the thin end of the wedge in terms of the activities and undertakings of Britain's extreme right.

The National Front

The National Front, largest and best known of Britain's extreme right parties, has since May 1979 seriously foundered; the setbacks it received in the General Election were severe and largely unexpected. Since that time the Front has undergone a dark and chaotic period of introspection and transition. But this transition will yield no significant transformation; metamorphosis will be merely cosmetic, or rather, tactical.

While it may be true that the National Front is to all intents and purposes a fascist organisation in essence, its tactical policy is largely opportunistic in character. Particularly in view of its recent experiences, the Front is developing the classic extremist 'two-track' strategy; while striving to establish a respectable reputation in the social and political domain by recanting or distancing itself publically from its past notoriety, the Front nevertheless is pursuing with redoubled vigour those associations and alliances in the domestic and international underground which incontrovertibly confirm its nazi and anti-social nature. The lesson learned in 1979 has induced the National Front yet further to broaden the distinction between the public image of 'print', and the covert commitment of 'practice'. As the *Sunday Telegraph* detected (5 March 1978), the Front's disavowal of racial hatred is a more than hollow device:

> The Front's policy on immigration is compulsory but 'humane' repatriation of all of Britain's population, accompanied by a massive programme of economic aid to the countries to which they return.
>
> This is not a picture which those who have attended National Front rallies will easily recognise.

The Front indeed has long been aware that the British electorate is not ready for fascism and, based upon that simple analysis, has concentrated on a policy of opportunism which, while falling short of a comprehensive world-view, seeks to provide simple and immediate solutions to complex and substantial problems. The opportunist feature has consistently proved the Front's corner-stone in the building of its popular support and it should not be forgotten in this context that the Front's first considerable impact was made in the aftermath of Enoch Powell's (in)famous 'Rivers of Blood' speech on the immigration issue in 1968.

But while expediency has largely directed the Front's public campaign, it has always issued from the well-spring of nazi ideology. At the same time however, the relationship between populism and polemic has traditionally been an uneasy one; ultimately, the fluidity of the one and the rigidity of the other contribute to a tension which is no longer profitable or tolerable. At these moments, the National Front, as with almost all other fascist groups and movements, has split and divided, hired and fired, regrouped and redefined. This in fact is currently the case with the Front, as the supposedly 'moderate' 'Constitutional Movement Within the Party' attempts to oust those leaders whose nazi and fascist reputations have unduly and for too long embarrassed the Front. The leadership struggle therefore is not only a fight for political dominance among personalities and factions, but also one whose outcome will determine the tactical success of the party in the immediate future. It is to be expected that recent trends will be confirmed and that populism will win the day over nazism, if only in terms of public consumption. But with every step that the National Front takes towards 'moderation' and popular appeal in its efforts to mobilise constituency and electoral support, so does it consolidate its more covert and sinister constituency of undiluted racism and nazism. The National Front is the non pareil 'Broad Church': its true nature lurks close at hand, though discreetly, under cover of its own monstrous shadow.

The development and sophistication of the 'two-track' strategy is well catalogued in the evolution of the National Front and its history as a party. No one with adequate memory or intelligence will believe that any of the figures involved prominently in the National Front, whatever their animosities and 'political differences', would be inclined to refashion the party in any mould that is not thoroughly fascist in shape and depth: the name-call of National Frontmen is the roll-call of post-war British fascism and nazism. Founded in 1967, the roots of the National Front are indeed firmly planted in the recent tradition of nazi groups. Six years after Sir Oswald Mosley founded the Union Movement, in 1948, A.K. Chesterton established his League of Empire Loyalists, the membership of which included Colin Jordan, John Bean, Martin Webster and John Tyndall. However, it was not until 1958 that race riots in Notting Hill and Nottingham leant any real encouragement to the far-right cause. Colin Jordan left the Empire Loyalists and formed his own White Defence League while John Bean and Andrew Fountaine set up their National Labour Party. By 1960, however, no real success had been encountered and the three entered an alliance through the formation of the British National Party, which, significantly, boasted a para-military elite corps under the joint direction of Jordan and John Tyndall; the unit was styled 'Spearhead', now transferred to Tyndall's National Front journal. But the overtly nazi displays of Tyndall and Jordan provoked a rift in the ranks of the BNP and the two broke away to form the National Socialist Movement, in which enlisted the youthful Martin Webster. By 1962, in alliance with Lincoln Rockwell's American nazi group, Jordan was proclaimed 'World Führer', presiding over a World Union of National Socialists. Tyndall, understandably perhaps disillusioned, left in 1964 to lead his own group, the Greater Britain Movement.

By 1966 however, it had become evident to the leading British fascists that their best efforts to mobilise mass popular support had gone largely unrewarded despite the fact that race relations and immigration had become real and crucial social issues. It was decided that the rag-bag of the right should be coordinated and galvanised; in 1967 the League of Empire Loyalists, the British National Party and the majority of the Racial Preservation Society merged and six months later were joined by Tyndall's Greater Britain Movement. Thus was born the National Front, 2000 in strength and with a pedigree unimpeachably nazi.

From the outset, the popular impulse was in conflict with fascist principle and nazi fantasy. Having exploited to the full the public controversy inspired by Enoch Powell's immigration speeches of 1968, the Front made its first modest electoral impression in the 1970 elections. But meanwhile the Front's first Chairman, A.K.

Chesterton, had resigned in protest at Tyndall's nazi activities, and in 1972 Chesterton's successor as Chairman, John O'Brien, had for similar reasons resigned his office. In the same year the Ugandan Asian crisis had stimulated National Front support to such a degree that Martin Webster achieved 16.2% of the poll at a West Bromwich bye-election, a proportion of votes never previously approached by a Front candidate in a Parliamentary election. In 1976, a National Front Local Government candidate in Leicester raised his share of the poll to 18%. Meanwhile, encouraged by the evident expansion of popular support, the party began to extend its platform to incorporate positions on, for instance, Northern Ireland, the Common Market, and 'law-and-order'. This extension of the platform accorded well with the 'two-track' strategy. Being for 'law and order' and against the 'Common Market' could be seen as 'respectable' in a way that racialism could not. Clearly it was intended that such new-found issues would provide a reputable and acceptable cloak for the more enduring but less palatable National Front platform. The Birmingham Stechford bye election campaign was accompanied by a proliferation of posters displayed in living-room windows calling for a rejection of the Common Market through the National Front vote. When questioned, many of these householders, while exhibiting scant knowledge of the EEC, nevertheless articulated clearly defined racist views.

Indeed the mid-1970s were a successful period for the National Front for the economic recession which beleaguered Britain at that time threw up exactly those social disaffections and difficulties which traditionally have profitted fascist organisations. The National Front asserted vigorously that economic hardships, inflation, unemployment, housing shortages, declining standards in education and welfare generally, the breakdown in law and order and all manner of associated problems were to be traced to the doors of black immigrants, and that only white British patriots, such as the National Front, could have the nation's best interests at heart. By 1974, the Front was able to field 90 candidates in the Autumn election and had thus passed the milestone of qualifying for free broadcast time on the media. But, at the same time, Tyndall's nazism had provoked further internal schism and he was ousted from his position as Chairman. In the following year he was expelled from the party itself but, following legal applications, was reinstated by the High Court. In response, the 'Populist' faction which had opposed him, broke away from the Front and, under the leadership

of John Kingsley Read, formed the short-lived National Party.
There then followed a period of consolidation during which
Tyndall, Webster and Andrew Fountaine set about moulding the
Front according to their own nazi-inspired vision, developing a
programme very much broader in scope than is realised by those
who see only the race issue as central to National Front
propaganda.

During the latter part of the 1970s the pattern continued; Tyndall
fought Webster, Tyndall and Webster fought Fountaine and Paul
Kavanagh. Successes in local elections, particularly in Greater
London, were followed by catastrophic failure in the 1979 General
Election; successful recruitment campaigns in the inner city areas
were at least arrested by the counter-campaigning strategy of the
Socialist Workers' Party-led Anti Nazi League. At the onset of the
1980s then, as suggested earlier, the National Front has come upon
a period of reassessment and regrouping. It lost a court action
over misrepresentation of usage of Excalibur House; party
membership has dropped dramatically; Fountaine and Kavanagh
were in the autumn of 1979 removed from the Executive having led an
abortive bid to oust Tyndall, who has himself been forced
subsequently to relinquish the chairmanship yet again, leaving his
enemy and ally Martin Webster in a dangerously exposed position.*
Meanwhile, Anthony Reed Herbert, while continuing to act as
National Front solicitor, has led a break-away faction out of the Front,
founding the British Democratic Party, and appropriating Front
properties in Nottingham and Leicester. In response, Tyndall has
himself formed the New National Front, complaining ironically in
what has become his own personal organ *Spearhead* (14 August
1980):

> What our enemies could not accomplish over 13½ years of unceasing
> endeavour had now been accomplished by the efforts of nationalists
> themselves: the NF has been smashed to pieces.

The National Front is clearly in a state of considerable confusion.
Ironically, however, many of the anti-Tyndall/Webster faction
welcome at least a degree of exposure of 'dirty linen', for an
apparent and public purge of nazi elements within the party will, in
their belief, facilitate the Front's eventual re-emergence as a
respectable party of the popular right. Reed Herbert's defection
therefore may be no more than a ruse through which to disassociate

---

* The current chairman of the National Front is Andrew Brons, a lecturer in Government and
Politics at Harrogate College of Further Education.

the 'moderate' faction from the 'nazis' until the way is clear to return to a pure and reputable party. However, as has been shown, the National Front has consistently been a party at odds with itself, not in terms of fundamental philosophy, so much as in its own attempts at self-representation and image-management. This latest crisis is not so convulsive as might appear to be the case. Once the lessons of 1979 have properly been absorbed and accommodated, and particularly if the party as a whole can assume a more anonymous, or at least less overtly nazi leadership, then the National Front will redirect its full and concerted energies towards its vision of a National Socialist Britain.

Primarily through the issue of 'racial priority', the National Front has identified the sections of society most susceptible to its propaganda, particularly the disadvantaged lower-middle class. This is the traditional target, according to David Edgar's 'Racism and Fascism and the Politics of the National Front' (*Race & Class*, No. 4), for fascism emerges as

> ... a counter-revolutionary mass movement during a period of capitalist crisis in which the conventional forces of the state are seen to be incapable of resolving the contradictions of the system. The participants in this mass movement tend to be drawn from those sectors of society ... which are facing a relative and progressive worsening of their economic and social position, but who nonetheless see no future in an alliance with the organised proletariat.

With this analysis in mind, and taking note of Joachim Fest's dictum that fascism represented 'a politically organised contempt for the mind', it is not hard to discern in the National Front a purely reactive and negative political and social impulse. Nevertheless, it is an impulse which will always find expression in periods in which the disadvantaged are most vulnerable, and as Peter Shipley rightly warns in his *Conflict Study* paper July 1978:

> Looking ahead, the fears and frustrations it exploits, especially the latent racialism, will not disappear overnight. In the event of renewed social or economic crisis, it may yet again begin to capture the allegiance of disaffected elements to a politically significant extent.

It is an impulse also which has not to date felt the inhibition of either accountibility or circumspection. As John Tyndall himself declared to the Front's 1977 Annual Conference:

> Our roots don't lie in arguments over abstractions of ideology or philosophy. Our roots lie in the simple values of *nation, race* and *country* ...

Our roots lie in the urge to *action*, in the will to get things done, in the determination to achieve what others only *talk* about.

Despite the Front's understandable 'urge to action' however, it has so far failed to express articulately its concept of the 'New Order' towards which it has set itself. It has on the other hand identified the enemies of that putative utopia, namely: all influences and causes which it considers to be subverting the civilisation of the white British nation, and especially Liberalism, Internationalism, Marxism and Zionism. Race and Politics are, in National Front thinking, inseparable; for political purity can be achieved only by the racially pure and 'unmongrelised'. Here again, the split-level of Front propaganda and fundamental nazism comes into play: as stated earlier, the immigration campaign is not a truly central issue but rather a devise and rallying-cry. Certainly, the Front intends to repatriate all coloured immigrants, 'honourably' and 'humanely' though compulsorily. Less explicit is its conviction that these immigrants are to be seen as passive agents in an international conspiracy, coordinated by World Jewry, to bring down and subjugate the traditional British order and white civilization in general. Indeed, ultimately John Tyndall's vision, as expressed at the 1977 Conference, owes very much more to nazi racial fantasy than to political reconstruction; his British dream is of 'a race striding the world like the colossus it once was – and stamping its power and its genius on the future pages of history.'

The impeccable nazism of John Tyndall may well prove to be his downfall as the National Front strives to redefine its popular image. But if Tyndall is obliged to relinquish his grip on Front affairs, one may not assume that the party has purged either its nazis or its nazism. Indeed, its politics betray the classic amalgam of Socialism, Nationalism and Racism. For example, in economic affairs the National Front depicts 'international finance capitalism' as the ruination of true British national interests. Not only is it obviously internationalist, but it also breeds a laissez-faire-liberal social attitude which in turn promotes and then tolerates Marxist intervention, for as its policy pamphlet asserts, 'finance capitalism breeds the conditions on which Red agitation thrives.' With a socialistic fervour, the Front's economic planners portray the financier as one who is 'nothing better than a huge parasite feeding on the body of the national economy and sustained by the labour of the people.' To complete the picture one need look no further than to the *Spearhead* magazine in which the editor Richard Verrall, the

Front's intellectual propagandist alleged to be the author of 'Richard E. Harwood's' *Did Six Million Really Die?*, insists blandly and with an almost disarmingly apologetic turn:

> If we are to consider the history of our times with genuine objectivity rather than a compulsion to be polite, we will have to admit that Zionist interests indeed preponderate in the powerful circles of international finance ...

The Front's 'Economic Nationalism' has approximately the same socialistic features and the same narrow objectives as had original Nazi economic planning, espousing strict state control while preserving the freedom of small business, in the 'national interest'. But its concept of the national interest anticipates a necessary and totalitarian control of the socio-economic order.

In short, it is evident that the National Front's plan to promote British freedoms is in practice more akin to a repression. While the thuggery of the Young National Front and the sedition of its paper *Bulldog* require no explication, Front policy on the Trade Unions is more ambivalent, and therefore more telling.

From its earliest days, the National Front has striven strenuously to infiltrate the unions and to reach particularly those on the factory floor who were economically most at risk and socially most disadvantaged. As was to be expected, the 'immigrant threat' was exploited not only as the cause of social and economic problems, but also as token of the political establishment's connivance at and indifference to the plight of the British working man, and its craven capitulation to 'alien' and international interests. Indeed, in 1978 the November issue of the AUEW journal carried a statement from Frontman Ray Broomhead which asserted:

> A high percentage of the membership of the AUEW would not support your anti-British pro-black, internationalist Labour Party if you paid them.

A year earlier, in 1977, the TUC had begun to take National Front intrusions seriously and instructed Trades Councils to exclude delegates active in fascist or racist organisations. By that time however, the Front had made considerable progress in the unions, particularly in those involving the Railways and the Post Office. Whenever possible, Front unionists were instructed to exploit latent shop-floor racism; the first major opportunity arose in 1972 in Loughborough when Asian workers went on strike at the Mansfield Hosiery factory; subsequently the Front involved itself in disputes at British Oxygen and at Imperial Typewriters, and latterly at the

Grunwick dispute. To galvanise these efforts a National Front Trade Union Association was established, its Industrial Affairs Committee being headed by Chairman Walter Barton of the EETPU, and Secretary Neil Farnell of the TGWU. On the one hand then, the National Front recognises the Unions as a recruiting-ground and a crucial political arena; according to John Tyndall:

... we have two alternatives: to be able to embark on a campaign of repression of the left in the unions, which could in the process involve the repression of much that is legitimate union activity, or win the battle in advance by winning control of the trade union movement by the normal democratic process.

Which particular alternative strategy is preferred by Tyndall himself was revealed succinctly and unambiguously in a speech to the Party Conference. So, on the other hand:

When we take over the reins of government, as one day we shall, these mobsters will find themselves in police cells so quickly they won't know what hit them.

Still less legitimate is the National Front's strategy of infiltrating the major political parties. As early after its formation as 1969, the National Front was advised through *Spearhead*'s columns by O.C. Gilbert, a pre-war member of the Imperial Fascist League:

I believe that the Conservative Party can be made much more right-wing by the infiltration tactics now operated by men like myself who for years have been members of the Conservative Party.

The Conservative Monday Club has been its particular target, and despite periodic purges within the Club, the National Front continues to attract or infiltrate right-wing Conservative circles. Indeed, as noted earlier, the Front is a broad church of the right. More than on one occasion it has acted as 'agent' for dissident elements of the Conservative Party. In 1970, for instance, the Northern League hosted a 'cultural' occasion, attended by ex-SS men, and, amongst others, members of both the National Front and the Monday Club. On another occasion, a Young Conservative was reported to have addressed a meeting of the Italian fascist party MSI with the greeting: 'I speak for the Monday Club, a British Fascist organisation.' There are many prominent figures on the extreme right who at one time or other had been Conservative Party members, even parliamentary candidates. Personalities such as the Dowager Lady Birdwood, editor of *Choice*, and G.K. Young have long been associated with activities on the right; Lady Jane Birdwood in particular does not appear to sense any compromise in her membership of the Conservative Party.

But, perhaps surprisingly, the National Front has not limited its 'entrist' activities to the Conservative Party. As recently as 1977 it was revealed that British Movement member Peter Marriner had not only contrived to infiltrate the Labour Party, but had even managed to become election agent for former MP Brian Walden at Birmingham Ladywood. He was subsequently appointed to act as agent for John Sever at the bye-election resulting from Walden's resignation, but was exposed and replaced by the late Bob Chamberlain. While acting as election agent, Marriner had also been more than active in, apart from the British Movement, the National Socialist Movement, the British National Party and the highly secretive outfit Column 88.

In terms of its own popular constituency, the National Front is strongest in London, followed by the West Midlands, Lancashire, South Yorkshire and the East Midlands. While the Front's appeal in Northern Ireland, Scotland and Wales has been inconsiderable, an offensive is currently being undertaken in Ulster, and contacts with the para-military UDA have long existed.

There are some 174 National Front Branches* throughout the UK, each presided over by a Committee of five under a Branch Organiser. Further, there are 21 Regional Councils responsible to a National Directorate of 20 members which runs eight departments overseeing the various aspects of policy and activities. The policy-making body is the six-man Executive Council. In addition to the monthly *Spearhead* magazine, the Front also produces a paper *NF News* and certain Branches or Regions distribute their own bulletins, for instance *Anglian News*.

As has been noted, the National Front has traditionally looked to the insecure and susceptible sections of the lower-middle class for support. The right-wing or radical intelligensia which had been attracted to Mosley's banner has to no significant degree been seduced by the less elitist and entirely unintellectual style of the Front. But until very recently, the Front was itself content to recruit where it could expect most immediate success and in those professions which it considered tactically and strategically crucial,

---

* A number of these have recently defected to one or other break-away group of the National Front.

for instance in the Territorial Army, the police and the prison service as well as in the key trade unions, the schools and latterly even in the churches. As the 1980s unfold however, the National Front is involving itself increasingly with the middle classes and the managerial professions. To a large degree this concern accounts for the anxiety within the Front over its nazi image. But the Front is also anticipating a fresh onslaught of recession which will begin more severely to erode the advantages and security of suburban Britain. The National Front's ability to exploit, as Peter Shipley put it, 'the fears and frustrations ... of disaffected elements', should not be underestimated. Whatever the transformation which is occuring in that party, be it in leadership, propaganda, style, even in name, the National Front remains and will remain a nazi inspired and racist organisation. If a National Front supporter is never sent to prison again for thuggery or desecration, it will be only because the party has learnt the strategy of the 'two-track' approach. However, it is more sure that National Front members will continue to practice illegalities, and, it is to be hoped, to be convicted for them. In May 1980, for instance, three men, two members, one of which was a former branch chairman, and a sympathiser, were convicted for an attempted arson attack on a printing works used by the Socialist Workers' Party. They had been detected owing to a crossed telephone line over which they were planning their mission.

If this account of the political nature of the National Front has not convinced the reader of its malevolent character, motives and ambitions, then it is hoped that the creature will be more certainly identified by the company that it keeps. For the National Front is intimately involved internationally with such groups as the Belgian VMO, the Dutch Volks Unie, the German NPD and Deutsche Burgerinitiative, the Italian MSI, the Spanish Cedade, the Norwegian Norsk Front, the French Nouveau Ecole, the Mexican Nazi Party, South African and Rhodesian organisations of the right, the American Ku Klux Klan, the States Right Party and the NSDAP-AO.

Despite differences of emphasis or of policy − the Front for instance is hostile in theory if not in practice to pan-Europeanism, a form of fascism which most other right-extremists espouse in Britain − the National Front maintains the closest contact and frequently merges its more sinister activities with most of the other less self-conscious parties of the British extreme right. Among these groups, accounts of which follow, the Front, despite animosities among the various leaderships, enjoys close operational and political relationships with the British Movement, the League of Saint George, the British League of Rights, Column 88 to name but the more prominent. With these international alliances and 'arrangements' in mind, it is certainly clear that the National Front is rather less National, rather more Front.

Other Extreme Parties of the Right

The formation, dissolution and fragmentation of extreme political groupings is so constant a characteristic of the ideological fringes as to render a comprehensive digest of extreme factions all but impossible. In addition, the ceaseless internal divisions, subversions and power struggles and the apparently 'peripatetic' nature of many of the more prominent personalities of the ultra-right all serve to inhibit total confidence in the reporting of the composition of the membership and leadership of the various factions. But the very fact that men like Colin Jordan, John Kingsley Read, John Tyndall and others seem at one time or another to have been directly involved in almost all of the far-right parties strengthens the conviction that the, albeit grudging, homogeneity of the right is a most significant feature and that the ceaseless dissolution and formation of factions represents a vulnerability which should not be overstated. Members of disintegrated parties do not generally return to the conventionally political fold; they either 'defect' to the more resilient groups, or set about styling new parties from what must be now a severely constricted catalogue of titles. One is indeed tempted to conclude from even a detailed scrutiny of some of the right-fringe parties that the chief distinction between them is one of ritual and is to be recognised in the ornamentation and emphasis of their activities: by, for instance, how many times annually, one or other group celebrates Adolf Hitler's birthday. 'Lunatic' as much of this attendant occultism and hero-worship may be, it should certainly not be dismissed. The cranks of the right are very serious people and for all their pretention and pantomime, their activities and ambitions are no less serious.

Two parties now defunct, the British National Party and the National Party, will serve as succinct examples of the 'broadness of association' of the far right and of the National Front's central, indeed pivotal, agency within that association.

A young nazi proudly displaying the various insignia of the British Movement.

The British National Party

The British National Party was originally formed in the early 1960s by Jordan, Bean and Fountaine and, through the activities of its para-military unit Spearhead led by Jordan and John Tyndall, speedily gained a reputation for nazism and violence. Jordan and Tyndall eventually broke away and gradually the BNP submerged. However, especially in view of later developments, it is worth noting a *Spearhead* directive of the early years which recommended to members:

> If you can't put on a uniform and get active, join a trade union or one of the three major parties. Become a dedicated member of the organisation, work hard and we will give leadership and keep your National Socialist spirit alive until you are needed.

In 1974 ex-National Frontman Eddie Morrison (who has recently rejoined the National Front) re-established the British National Party in Leeds, basing its constituency on the decayed National Democratic Movement. Though its membership was always small, it nevertheless acquired a reputation for being both active and violent. Its publication *British News* advocated the setting up of White Defence Associations and described the BNP's function as that of 'oiling the fascist machine'. Accordingly BNP members participated with the Nazi Party UK and Column 88 in the Nazi Muster Camp of 1975 and maintained close contact with an assortment of sympathetic groups including the National Party, the British Movement and the League of Saint George.

When the BNP once more passed into oblivion in the late 1970s its 'Final Bulletin' in what is merely an extension of the earlier *Spearhead* directive, advised members:

> ... join the National Front, we feel this is where our future lies. The great work we have done will not be wasted. We join a larger, more efficient organisation, within which we can carry on the fight. No one will be forced to change or alter their ideas as the NF has emerged as a truly radical and viable political movement.

Whether the motive of this advice is towards entrism or merely collaboration, it is clear that when the going gets tough, British nazis are inclined to seek the shelter of the National Front not only as a refuge but also with confidence for the future of British fascism.

The National Party

The National Party is a complementary example for it is that of a faction which, in 1975/6, under the direction of John Kingsley Read, split off from the National Front in order to 'lose' the nazi image. As a populist party, the National Party devoted its attention to the electoral process, but could not resist the temptation of illegitimate tactics. In fact, the National Party collapsed in October 1977 following disclosures of election irregularities involving NP man John Frankman who was obliged to resign his seat on the Blackburn Council.

As for the National Party's avowed recanting of nazism – it should be noted that extreme right objections usually find fault not so much in the substance of nazism as in its public parade – this criticism did not inhibit it from close contact with such parties as the nazi National Youth Alliance of America and the West German National Democratic Party (the NPD). The National Party's own journal *Britain First* frequently reprinted articles from other undeniably nazi journals and in fact the League of Saint George's *League Review*, reporting on a speech delivered by Kingsley Read in 1977 in which he suggested that he had much in common with members of the British National Party, very fittingly reveals the National Party's brand of 'moderation':

> ... even if nationalists disagreed among themselves as to tactics, if we agreed that we were all nationalists, then we should work together.

It is wholly unsurprising therefore, that following their somewhat tepid and ultimately abortive flirtation with legitimacy, many members of the collapsed National Party returned to the more sheltered fold of the National Front.

John Kingsley Read himself went on to form the Democratic Nationalist Party which attracted meagre support. Such was his disillusionment, that in 1979 he announced, somewhat ingenuously, that he was retiring from political life in order to return to university where he hoped to study community work.

The parties and factions of the right can usefully be divided into two categories: the 'hard men' and the propagandists. Right of the National Front there are few pretensions to any order of moderation, and, at times, little regard for discretion. However, many of the organisations, particularly the para-military units, are extremely secretive and highly and elaborately security-conscious.

Information is hard to come by, but the evidence which investigations have yielded provides a clear enough picture of the composition and activities of these groups. The propagandists obviously have no intention of obscuring their message, though often their motives are strenuously disguised. However, while it is not difficult to acquire extremist literature, it is not always so easy to trace its source. One fact is indeed a truism: that when enquiry becomes problematic, its closely guarded object becomes the more interesting, not to say sinister.

The British Movement

The British Movement was formed in 1968 by Colin Jordan, who until 1975 was its Chairman. He was obliged to resign however on conviction of having attempted to shoplift a box of chocolates and items of ladies' underwear from a branch of Marks and Spencers. Since his successor Michael McLaughlin took over, membership has more than doubled to a level of about 1500, organised in some 25 branches nationwide and particularly strong on Merseyside and in the West Midlands.

The British Movement has a small Women's Division and publishes two regular journals, *British Patriot* ('The Voice of White Britain') and *British Tidings* ('Bulletin of the British Movement'). Its regulating National Council has included such noteworthy individuals as Peter Marriner, Albert Chambers, Terry Pearson, David Cooper, Richard Middleton, Mike Noonan, Arthur Shorthouse and Brian Baldwin, now of the National Front but a man with broad experience in the British National Party, the League of Saint George and Unit 88 of Column 88 as well as the British Movement. Of particular concern is the fact that Baldwin is also the Chairman of the Prison Officers Association at Strangeways Prison in Manchester. As John Tyndall told a journalist on the *Western Independent*:

> We do have a larger than average number of supporters of the National Front among prison officers. We are particularly strong at Strangeways, Pentonville and the Scrubs.

Derek Merry, former National Front organiser and self-confessed UDA recruiter added:

> There is a National Front cell amongst some officers at Dartmoor Prison

though I am not prepared to say how many of them there are. They exist as a separate body really but we prefer that to them not existing at all.

The extra-curricula activities of many of these prison officers is a very serious matter of concern, not least for those black, Jewish and Muslim prisoners in their custody. Both inside and outside, the British Movement's commitment to all kinds of violent racial hatred is well documented, and indeed, scarcely concealed. The Movement's efforts to render Britain a 'No Go Area for further immigrants' has frequently fallen foul of the law; one singularly nasty tactic employed in such campaigns has been the booby-trapped leaflet stuck to a wall and concealing a razor blade which slashes the fingers of anyone attempting to remove the sticker. Anti-Semitism is also a British Movement trade-mark. As former National Council member Richard Middleton boasted to the *News of the World* (18 December, 1977):

> We ran into some Jews at Hoxton market and put six of them in hospital. The others fled. A Jew's jaw came into contact with a Leader Guard's boot.

The British Movement's relationship with the National Front has always been ambivalent. Colin Jordan, who in 1980 resurrected Arnold Leese's *Gothic Ripples* bulletin and who was during 1979 making an attempt to regain favour in the BM and in the National Reorganisation Party which is run by BM men Richard Middleton, Steven Goodier and Ian Millard, was no doubt prompted by the Front's internal problems to castigate 'the Jew-infiltrated phony facade known as the "National Front" ':

> It was never the great herald of a golden future, and now the best that can happen to it is for it to be given a decent burial so that it can no longer side-track people from the only real force of regeneration which has won in the past and can and will win again in the future – National Socialism.

Michael McLaughlin shares this disparagement of the populist effort; under his control the British Movement makes no secret of its allegiance to Nazism and takes no real interest in the more subtle politics of the electoral canvass. As he wrote in the BM journal *British Patriot*:

> ... unlike the National Front, we don't hide behind hypocrisy. We'd rather die with our souls intact ...

On the other hand, the British Movement is not above appearing on National Front platforms, attending meetings and manoeuvres with

Anti-Semitism – a British Movement trade mark.

Front members, sharing logistic resources, and accepting NF sponsorship in the form of funds. British Movement man Rod Roberts was responsible in part for the redirection of Front monies to the British Movement. On 20 January 1981, Roberts was jailed for seven years on charges of arson, possession of arms and ammunition, including a sten gun, an anti-riot gun, revolvers and rifles, and an offence against the Race Relations Act. Also convicted were BM colleague Harvey Stock and five others.

The British Movement has extensive foreign contacts and having split, along with the Belgian VMO, from the fascist coordinating body the 'New European Order' has now formed a rival organisation 'Europa'. It is affiliated to the World Union of National Socialists, the Führer of which was once Colin Jordan, and to the White Peoples' Alliance, through which it maintains links with the Ku Klux Klan. It has also close relations with the American NSDAP-AO Nazi Party, with the Spanish Cedade organisation, with the Belgian Rexists, the French FANE, the notorious Turkish Grey Wolves, with Italian, German and Austrian groups, and particularly with the singularly vicious Flemish Militant Order (the VMO). Indeed contacts and alliances between the British Movement, the VMO and German nazi groups are intimate enough to be of considerable concern to the West German Interior Ministry. In the 1978 edition of its *Verfassungsschutz*, a survey of extremist groups considered to comprise a threat to democratic security in West Germany, the Ministry takes careful note of these British Movement involvements.

The British Movement's inclination towards 'militarism' is a slender secret. Recruitment drives are periodically directed at the TAVR and Cadet Forces and both institutions have in the past been infiltrated. Selected BM members are recruited into the 'Leader Guard' in which they receive uniforms and 'special training'. In the August/September 1976 issue of *British Patriot*, the BM ominously counselled its members:

> The British Movement ... encourages its members to join the Territorial Army, Britain's part time army. It does so on the assumption that the crime rate, and in particular, crimes of a political nature are likely to increase and envisages the formation of a 'Free Corp' should the government's forces cease to maintain stability.

Whatever the express purposes of such a *Frei Korps*, it would certainly not be to defend the liberal status quo. As Richard

Law and Order and the British Right

Middleton told the *News of the World*:

> We're not a democratic party ... when we get power we will have our own solutions to immigrants ... the final solution.

In fact the Leadership Guard is not inexperienced in battle conditions. The British Movement has long provided mercenary units for foreign wars, notably against the Marxist forces in the Angolan conflict of the middle 1970s. It will be remembered that BM men and VMO members were captured by TV news cameras as they scurried across international airports en route for Africa and that some of them even now languish in Angolan jails. The British Movement is after the National Front the largest extreme right party in Britain. Financially it seems adequately equipped. Apart from National Front support, its 'British Patriots Publications' operation and its sale of other literature, films, tapes, records and militaria bring in as much as £800 per month. Foreign funding, notably from groups in the USA and South Africa further supplement BM's income.

The League of Saint George

The League of Saint George, despite its fanciful and folkish title, is one of the especially sinister organisations on the extreme right. It regards itself as elite among nazis and from that eminence, is prone rather to despise the 'street-fighting' capacity of both the National Front and the British Movement. This condescension however, does not prevent it from infiltrating those groups in order to influence policy and activity, or from recruiting members from its rivals. Indeed, though ironically the National Front has proscribed the League on account of its comparative 'extremism', many NF members simultaneously hold membership of that body and the *League Review* frequently carries articles penned by NF leaders. The League has also assumed a role in the leadership struggles within the National Front and has leant considerable support to the cause of Paul Kavanagh in his efforts to unseat Tyndall and Webster, whom the League believes to be responsible for the Front's diminished success. However, should Webster survive, the League have laid contingency plans which include a somewhat closer alliance with the British Movement.

The League of Saint George was founded in 1974 by a number of disaffected members of the Union Movement who did not idolise Sir

Oswald Mosley and who found his own particular anti-Semitism distastefully moderate. Originally based in North London, the League now claims nationwide membership particularly among the middle class and professionals. There are several discrete levels within the League, the top-most of which is alone privileged to know the League's organisational and operational secrets. The leadership itself is a small select group which includes President Herbert Grestock, Membership Secretary Mike Griffin, International Affairs Officer Steven Brady, and others, such as Keith Thompson, Leslie Vaughan, Clive Lucas and Don Sayer, all experienced and hardened extremists.

The League produces a glossy bi-monthly review, the *League Review*, well constructed and well written and with an emphasis on subtle racism. The League's book club, Sunwheel Distributors, sells a wide range of Nazi and racist 'classics'.

As a supplement to its interest in 'patriotism' the League practices the cult of Odinism, which, its adherents believe, is a faith which binds together all Northern European types throughout the world. Founded upon Norse and Celtic mythology and upon an idolatry of the Norse war god, Odinism is a practice both occult and fear-inducing and is embraced and exploited by several of the ultra-right groups which are attracted by the strategic notion of order through fear. In the past Colin Jordan and Andrew Fountaine of the National Front have espoused the cult which is largely promoted by The Northern League and its publication *The Northlander*, by the Odinist Committee of London and its publication *Raven Banner* and by Paul Jarvis' Viking Youth which publishes *Young Folk*. According to *Raven Banner* this primitive and superstitious form of paganism represents 'a return to the heroic, idealistic philosophy of our age' – a sentimentality which does not particularly accord with the League of Saint George's view, as expressed in the *League Review* (1976, No. 11), that 'events of catastrophic proportions will rapidly overtake civilization.'

Somewhat naively, the League of Saint George seeks to describe itself as a 'non-party, non-sectarian political club' with the aim of promoting 'patriotic' European cultural principles of society against the Communist threat.

In pursuance of this end however, the League has pledged itself:

1. to spread the National Socialist ideology through activities and propaganda;

2. to achieve a European union of 'Nationalists';
3. to coordinate international activities of sympathetic groups;
4. to galvanise the efforts of British fascist groups;
5. to act as an umbrella organisation servicing the fascist movement.

Apart from the usual film-shows and Hitler birthday parties, the League regularly engages in para-military training and briefings at secret special camps, often in association with members of other extremist groups both domestic and foreign. In fact, with the aid of the British Movement, the League coordinates the British fascists' annual pilgrimage to Diksmuide in Belgium at which rally it is now the official British representative. Hosted jointly by the Flemish VMO and the Langemark SS, the Diksmuide excursion honours the Belgian nazi collaborators killed fighting for the Third Reich, and is attended by nazis from throughout Europe and further afield. The mid-summer 1980 Diksmuide rally was particularly well represented by British nazi contingents, among them members of the British Movement, Viking Youth, the League of Saint George, Column 88 and the National Front. Prominent individuals included

No escape from Nazism even in death.

Stephen Brady the former school teacher (until convicted of assault), who is now a leading League member, Peter Marriner, former Labour Party agent, now a leader of both the British Movement and Column 88 and his colleague Raymond Hill founder of the National Front in South Africa, Martin Wingfield, a National Front organiser, convicted in 1979 for an assault upon a Jewish cafe-owner, and Mary Downton, membership secretary of the British League of Rights who told a *News of the World* reporter:

> I want to see a Fourth Reich and we all want the blacks and Jews out of this country.

Also in attendance was Mary Downton's daughter Sheila, secretary of the Petts Wood 'Young Conservatives'.

Apart from the traditional parades, marches and pledges, there also took place a top-level meeting between the various paramilitary groups, including Column 88, the UDA and other British groups, to plan concerted strategy against the 'common enemy'. The outrages of August, September and October 1980 perpetrated in Bologna, Munich and Paris, in which about 100 people lost their lives, may well have been coordinated at Diksmuide.

The League itself has long-established understandings with a veritable host of neo-nazi groups from every country in Western Europe, from Canada and the USA, from Argentina and Australia, from New Zealand and South Africa. Principal contacts include the Ku Klux Klan and the National States Rights Party and the NSDAP-AO of the USA, the Volks Unie and Nazi Northern League from Holland, the German Deutsche Burgerinitiative, the French FANE, and the Flemish VMO itself.

As if the activities of the League of Saint George were not wide enough, the League also acts as a screen and recruiting base for the highly clandestine unit Column 88 the membership of which, highly selective as it is, includes the majority of the League's leadership.

Column 88

Column 88 — the 88 signifies the eighth letter of the alphabet, HH for *Heil Hitler* — was formed in 1970 out of the debris of the National Socialist Group and in reaction to Colin Jordan's supposed betrayal of the ultra-militant right when in 1968 he dropped the name 'National Socialist' in the face of the race relations laws.

As mentioned earlier, Column 88 recruits with the utmost of caution and applies the strictest criteria in its selection process. It demands not only ideological orthodoxy, but also a high standard of technical ability in intelligence work, arms handling and the use of explosives. It is therefore not surprising that investigations indicate that the Column has not only infiltrated the TAVR, but has also established contacts in the regular army. Apparently, its access to efficient training techniques and weaponry is considerably facilitated through this penetration. Recruits are rigorously screened before being allotted to their cell. The chain of command is complicated and intentionally obscured even from cell-members who may win promotion only through rigorous application, achievement and merit. Instructions are transmitted to the cells by tape-recordings, one of which declares to Column units:

> Column 88 should be seen and understood as an advanced guard, a special force sent into territory that was abandoned years ago to the enemy.

To that end, Column 88 has carried out a series of postal bomb attacks as well as 'raids' on left-wing bookshops though its chief function has to date been the provision of security services to right-wing causes in general.

But Column 88 undertakes stringent and comprehensive guerilla training programmes and maintains contact with active terrorist units in Italy and with Palestinian groups through which are channeled Arab financial contributions to supplement funding received from domestic groups and from wealthier European nazi parties.

According to the anti-fascist journal *Searchlight*, Column 88 has broad ambitions:

> Their long term objectives are to have their members in places of influence across the whole spectrum of the Right, from Monday Club to the National Front, and to slowly but surely make sure National Socialism is not only not forgotten but also edges ahead bit by bit within these groups.

This analysis is admirably confirmed by a letter emanating from code-name 'Langemarck' at Column 88 HQ England, and addressed 'Dear Racial Comrade':

> I do not need to tell you that we too, in Britain, cherish the National Socialist tradition of preserving the longest possible memory – in order that

we may both maintain the honoured standard of Blood Loyalty to our proven friends when they are in adversity; and equally, that we may continue to demonstrate to the World the merciless account with which we shall present our Enemies when the time for settlement has come ... WIR KOMMEN WIEDER

Less grandiose and rhetorical, and a great deal more specific as to the activities of Column 88 is the following communication, 'Top Secret' and intended for 'trusted Group Leaders ONLY'. Dated 2 March 1977 it comes from M.D. Barnett (Major) of the 1st Battalion No. 4 Unit (Nordic Para-Military Unit No. 4):

The next military exercise will take place on an arranged and isolated area of Salisbury Plain over the Easter period. It is hoped to have *trusted* observers from a number of right-wing groups from the UK and the Continent. The exercise will consist of field operations and also how to deal with left-wingers and organisers when our time comes. Following our recent visit to Germany, we have now arranged for a similar exercise to take place in northern Germany during the summer.

Our recent problems with the VMO are now overcome so we can resume our activities with them in due course. Our arms supply is now first class, and with the cooperation of some serving officers in the Regular Army, who are at last coming around to our way of thinking, our position will soon be most encouraging.

Such evidence speaks for itself. Column 88 however, is not the only such 'Special Section'.

SS Wotan 18

SS Wotan, known also variously as the 11th Hour Brigade, the Adolf Hitler Commando Group, the Iron Guard, the Knights of the Iron Cross and the Dirlwanger Brigade, has also been responsible for fire-bombing attacks on minority communities and left-wing properties.

Again, as with Column 88, its members are steeped in Nordic myth, occultism and Hitler-worship. More significantly it also has a considerable stockpile of arms, including Armalite rifles, Mills grenades, Carl Gustav anti-tank guns and other modern and sophisticated weaponry.

Principal organisers of the unit include David Wilson, Michael Noonan who was formerly head of the British Movement's Leader Guard, and John Knight and his wife Primrose who once contrived to infiltrate the Socialist Workers' Party.

Wotan, whose existence came to light in 1976, produces a monthly journal *Adler und Kreuz* and while highly secretive, maintains a slightly higher profile than Column 88, and contains a broader-based membership. It is highly likely that Wotan actually acts as a testing-ground and vetting service for Column 88. But there is no doubt as to its own particular agency and capacity, or to its purpose.

The groups and parties of the ultra-right so far discussed constitute the 'advanced guard' of British fascism, literally as well as politically. Sheltering in the rear are ranked the sedition-mongers and propagandists, so many little Goebbels behind so many little Himmlers — as yet no equivalent little Hitler has risen from the lower depths of British nazism.

Most of these 'secondary' groups assume one or other thin disguise, as 'special interest' academic publicists, as anti-communist vigilantes, as democratic lobbyists, or simply as legitimate rightist pressure groups. The interested party need only glance at the literature for which these organisations are responsible, or scan their membership, to arrive at less impeccable a description.

The British League of Rights

In an interview with the *Guardian* (25 February 1980), the editor of *Searchlight* Maurice Ludmer drew attention to the relative success of low-profile propagandists on the right:

> He has given some attention to two organisations, Tory Action and The League of Rights, which, he claims have embedded themselves inside a section of the Conservative Party. He says they are racist and anti-semitic, dedicated to repatriation among other things. He keeps an eye on the spate of para-military retired generals who appeared during the 1974 crisis, talking darkly of strong government, and even, he claims, armed intervention in politics ...
> ... He reckons on a rough head count that about 12 Conservative MPs would be a push-over if any ultra right-wing group were to make any political headway. ·

With these strictures in mind, it is indeed salutory to note that the official patron of the British League of Rights is a retired military man, Air Vice-Marshall Donald Bennett, and prominent within the League's ranks is the ubiquitous Dowager Lady Birdwood, a longstanding member of the Conservative Party. Bennett is indeed a dignitary with broad right-wing connections, most of which have been discreetly disguised. However, his patronage of the British League of Rights is openly canvassed in his 1979 *Who's Who* entry. In the 1960's he was involved in the rightist 'anti-communist' New Liberal Party, more recently in the 'Safeguard Britain Campaign' which, equipped with its paper *Market News*, was pledged against the EEC, but whose links with the League of Rights somewhat impaired its credentials. Indeed so staunchly did Bennett oppose Britain's membership of the Common Market, as did the National Front, that he at one time offered a substantial amount of money to sympathetic lobbies and was in fact moved to present himself as United Anti-Common Market candidate in the Cotswolds constituency at the 1979 elections for the European Parliament. He achieved 6% of the vote, without widely disclosing his own distinct political leanings. Apart from these activities and his patronage of the League, the Air Vice-Marshall also runs the isolationist British Independence Movement. The catalogue of Lady Birdwood's affiliations is inclusive, if not catholic.

The British League of Rights was established in 1970 by Donald A. Martin who had long been active in the Australian League of Rights whose avowed aim from the outset has been to secure the service of 'opinion-moulders' and whose strategy to this end has incorporated successful infiltration of various Australian institutions, not least the Liberal Party. The British League was formed with similar objectives in mind and, as noted, has met with some success in the Conservative Party. According to *Searchlight* (No. 49), the League engages in two levels of penetration:

> ... those which are simply front organisations for the League of Rights, and those whose origins were independent of the League but which have been the focus of the League's declared aim of winning over the 'opinion moulders' and which have come to be heavily influenced by the League or its supporters.

The League's monthly journal *On Target* is generally careful not to offend the sensibilities of the right-wing Conservatives whom it wishes to influence or enlist. Little by little however, a less than orthodox political tendency emerges. The Labour Party is, the journal claims, 'an isolated Marxist intellectual party without mass support', one which 'can one day and without difficulty be firmly crushed by a patriotic government.' Yet more revealing is the League's classic fascist attitude towards 'the link between "Big Finance" and Communism'. To complete the picture, Don Martin reviewed the TV serial *Holocaust* in the *On Target* journal; it was, he wrote:

> ... a massive and most costly psychological warfare exercise ... set in motion over the entire globe by Zionism's network of innumerable clandestine organisations.

A brief scrutiny at the list of titles distributed through the League's literature outlet Bloomfield Books, owned by Don Martin, confirms this nazi obsession with Conspiracy Theory and anti-Semitism. The list includes such titles as *The Hoax of the Twentieth Century* which denies the genocide of the final solution, *Learned Elders and the BBC* which alleges a Jewish conspiracy to control the media, *The Talmud Unmasked* which enlarges the conspiratorial ambitions of world Jewry, *Racial Integration* which warns of the evils of race mixing and 'mongrelisation'.

The League's activities and interests are by no means limited to domestic issues and campaigns; its foreign and overseas contacts are many and various. It is federated to the Crown Commonwealth League of Rights and also, since 1974, has been the British chapter of the World Anti-Communist League, described by former Conservative MP Geoffrey Stewart-Smith when, in 1974, he withdrew his Foreign Affairs Circle from WACL's membership, as 'a hot-bed of anti-Jewish intrigue.' Certainly the League of Rights, or League for European Freedom as it is discreetly known within WACL, has not served to moderate the World Anti-Communist League's image. Indeed quite the opposite has occurred as Martin himself complained in *On Target*:

> Ever since the League of Rights and similar organisations joined the World Anti-Communist League ... there has been an international campaign to smear WACL.

The *Washington Post*, presumably contributing to this 'campaign', noted that at WACL's 1978 Conference, 'forces were stirring within the WACL — forces of authoritarianism, neo-fascism, racial hierarchy and anti-Semitism.'

The stirring of these 'forces' will surprise no commentator familiar with the motives and inspirations of WACL's affiliated members which, apart from the 'League for European Freedom', include the Italian MSI party, the Spanish Cedade and the Mexican right-wing terrorist group Tecos. Perhaps of still greater concern, if in itself not entirely unexpected, is the fact that WACL is heavily financed by the governments of Taiwan, Saudi Arabia and South Korea.

11,422 electors in the Cotswolds cast their votes for Air Vice-Marshall Bennett's United Anti-Common Market platform; the number of them who were, or are, aware of their candidate's political pedigree would be considerably smaller.

The Self-Help Organisation and Choice

When in 1974 the British League of Rights succeeded the Foreign Affairs Circle as British chapter of WACL, Don Martin conferred upon Lady Jane Birdwood the office of General Secretary of the League for European Freedom. This is not the only distinction that Lady Jane Birdwood has achieved in ultra right-wing politics. Indeed in 1970, she formed an organisation of her own. Self-Help was ostensibly conceived as an anti-Trade Union lobby, not entirely unlike the National Association for Freedom (or Freedom Association as it is now known). Self-Help involved itself in the tumultuous union disputes at Grunwick and at the Randolph Hotel in Oxford, as did NAFF. Both organisations, in expressing concern or outrage at what they interpret as undue union influence in national politics, have devised their various blue-prints or consultation documents for an alternative labour-relations strategy; Self-Help's is comprehensive. Lady Jane Birdwood's paper *British Gazette* proposes the mobilisation of massive strike-breaking facilities, encompassing the organisation of special funds, stockpiles of industrial and consumer supplies, an alternative transport system nationwide and a national daily news bulletin. Already, Self-Help has equipped itself with a radio-communications network, albeit of rudimentary proportions, in anticipation no doubt of an imminent leftist coup. Meanwhile Self-Help announces in its national advertising campaign:

> We could permeate the Conservative Party and give it backbone.

The kind of 'backbone' which Lady Jane Birdwood provides the Conservative Party already is sufficiently distorted to be of grave concern to members of that party who cherish more orthodox interpretations of their manifesto. The National Association for Freedom may be described as 'radical right' Tory; many of the other rightist pressure groups with which Lady Jane Birdwood is associated may be described as somewhat right of radical. Another of Lady Jane Birdwood's operations, the Choice Organisation, which she chairs, is more specific in its direction. Hoping to raise some £1,500,000 in furtherance of its anti-immigration campaign, the Choice committee produced a broadsheet whose thesis and rhetoric bear a distinctly National Front house-style. Referring to the 'immigrant scroungers', *Choice* states:

> In our minds there would appear to be no valid reason why we should continue to quench their insatiable thirst, thereby impoverishing ourselves, and reducing Britain herself to Third World status.

In conclusion the rather inappropriately styled Choice committee asserts:

> (the) white electorate has no alternative but to call for a national referendum in order to register its unequivocal opposition to the wholesale destruction of our national identity and social order.

Choice is of course only one of several 'populist' anti-immigration lobbies which in recent years have attracted publicity and support. Others include Tory Action, The Immigration Control Association, led by Joy Page and Mary Howarth, the British Campaign to Stop Immigration led by Jim Merrick and the Conservative Monday Club's Halt Immigration Now Campaign. There is also the apparently respectable Clarendon Club which presents itself as a sort of after-dinner debating society and which holds its functions at exclusive London hotels. In reality it is a fund-raising enterprise for the extreme right and is patronised by such distinguished speakers as Stephen Brady of the UDA, the League of Saint George, and Column 88, former National Front directorate member Tony Webber and others including at least two civil servants at the Ministry of Defence, an ex-SAS officer and other military men. More than one meeting has been addressed by the unconventional historian David Irving, author of controversial re-evaluations of the Second World War and its personalities.

The Racial Preservation Society

If the British League of Rights is an anti-communist organisation, if Self-Help promotes free enterprise and if Choice seeks to preserve the national identity, it is indeed impossible to describe the function of the Racial Preservation Society, another group with which Lady Jane Birdwood has been intimately involved. Initially a propaganda operation, the RPS is perhaps the most sinister and sordid of Britain's specifically racist lobbies. It was formed in 1964; three years later the majority of its members joined in the formation of the National Front. But in 1974, the RPS re-emerged in Brighton among the members of the Northern League, a nazi-cultural society focused on the more sophisticated and legendary aspects of racism, nazi cultism, Aryanism, Odinism and Hitler-worship.

The RPS came into existence through a meeting between the owners of the 'Heidelberg' Hotel in Brighton, the Hancock family, a local Conservative Jimmy Doyle, Raymond Bamford a wealthy heir and Robin Beauclaire, a wealthy businessman with extreme right-wing leanings. Funds were raised, including donations from senior Civil Service and Military men, and two papers, *RPS News* and *British Independent*, were launched nationally. However, following a series of complaints against the contents of these publications, Hancock and others, including a Rhodesian agent of the illegal Smith regime, were prosecuted at Lewes under the terms of the Race Relations Act. The action failed, much to the delight of the British right. (In the spring 1978 however, Hancock pleaded guilty to the possession of a prohibited firearm, offered no defence in court, and was fined £300.)

The Racial Preservation Society next set itself to infiltrate the local Conservative Party and the Monday Club. But the strategy's chief architect Jimmy Doyle was arrested and convicted on a charge involving possession of stolen antiques and Monday Club connections were exposed. (Doyle had a previous conviction for an assault on a police officer.) The RPS had not only been flirting with the Conservative Party fringe, but also with the Northern League, Column 88 and with such individuals as Colin Jordan and Martin Webster.

By 1977 however, the RPS was back in business and distributing a new publication *Race and Nation*. The Hancocks were still very much involved as was Ted Budden and former NF Directorate member Denis Pirie. The Hancocks own the printing-press on which the NF's *Spearhead* journal was printed as well as several commissions undertaken for Robin Beauclaire's Historical Review Press. Beauclaire who has had connections with most of the extreme parties of the right over the last fifteen years, is a self-confessed anti-Semite responsible for the publication of several works of the most virulent order of white-supremacist and anti-Semitic racism. Included among these works are A.R. Butz's *The Hoax of the*

Twentieth Century and Richard Harwood's *Did Six Million Really Die?* both of which deny the actuality of the Holocaust.

While the Racial Preservation Society and the Historical Review Press may be entirely disreputable, other such organs of racist theory are promulgated under an aura of pseudo-academic respectability; the German *Neue Anthropologie*, the French *Nouvelle Ecole* and the British *Mankind Quarterly* are related publications, all fronted by supposedly eminent academics who, in one way or another, subscribe to a 'scientific' racist theory. The overall editor of the British journal since its first edition in 1960, Professor R. Gayre was in fact a key witness for the defence at the Lewes Trial of RPS members. Having alluded to the 'scientific evidence' for the racial inferiority of the negro peoples, he was moved to contribute £25 towards the defence fund with the bland justification:

> I think one should be able to discriminate on the grounds of race and colour.

Such subtle and pseudo-intellectually couched racism, and especially latterly anti-Semitism, have made a considerable impression on less critical minds in search of simple explanations to complex problems. The demand for the pamphlet *Did Six Million Really Die?* has, on an international scale, been quite staggering. As Maurice Ludmer explained to the *Guardian*:

> I haven't been able to detect a real political theory. ... They realise they are all tarred with the Nazi brush. We have too many pictures of Tyndall and the others dressing up in uniforms, and listening to Hitler tapes, for them to escape that image. So now they are teaching people that the Nazis didn't really kill the Jews. It was just a Jewish propaganda conspiracy after the war.

(The groups here described represent the more significant organisations on the extreme political right. There are others: The Action Party founded by Sir Oswald Mosley and led by Jeffrey Hamm with a monthly journal *Action*; the National Socialist Group; the National Socialist Party UK; the National Independence Party; the National Assembly; Britannia Party; Freedom Party; Campaign Against Communism; National Reorganisation.)

There is no mistake to be made; whatever their particular and identifying emphasis or activity, with or without a 'real political theory', the parties of the extreme right are in broad agreement. Having rewritten the past, they would, given the opportunity, forcefully strive to recreate the future.

The Left

Trotskyism and Entrism

It is no less 'Augean' a task to prepare an accurate compilation of the parties of the extreme left, as it is of the right. No sooner has one completed one's account than two parties merge, three collapse, four re-style themselves and five spawn factions, fractions and tendencies. However, while factionalism on the right is frequently the outcome of personal rivalries and internal power-struggle, leftist schism owes more to the obscure and tortuous redefinition and reinterpretation of ideology and strategy which is so constant a feature in revolutionary politics. By extension, as Paul McCormick points out in *Enemies of Democracy*, it is also a highly problematic proposition to place the various factions of the left in any permanent relationship to the democratic political process:

> Sometimes a rough division is made between those Marxists who seek to 'smash the system' – the system including the established institutions and bodies like Parliament, the Labour Party, and the trade unions, and those who seek to 'work within the system' to change it into a Marxist system ... Groups drift in and out of different tactical positions. One day a group may be working within the system genuinely, believing that it can achieve success within it. The next day the same group may be working within the system insincerely, using the system to sabotage it from within. Later on the same group will be operating outside the system.

Certainly the tactical attitude which extreme left groups have towards the institutions of democracy gives rise to considerable confusion, even within their own ranks. The 'entrist' strategy gave way in the late 1960s to a less covert involvement in national politics; but, having failed electorally to exploit the disaffections and disillusionments induced by the recession of the mid-1970s, the left is reconsidering the advantages of 'low-profile' politics. The Militant Tendency in particular has both strategically and conceptually grasped the lesson of recent political experience. As Peter Mair

A Trotskyist group, the Spartacist League, expressing 'solidarity' with coloured immigrants. Brick Lane, 1979.

explains in his essay in *Multi-Party Britain*, (edited by H.M. Drucker):

> Electoral disenchantment with the major parties does not in itself imply greater political opportunities for the Marxist left. Unlike, say, the Liberals, the left is simply not an alternative party (or parties) which can hope to exploit any disintegration in the two-party system. Rather, the Marxist left represents another system of politics, ideologically and in some cases organisationally divorced from the political culture of British political democracy. To transfer one's political loyalty from Labour to the Liberals is not the same as transferring from Labour to the Marxist left.

This is precisely the point that has struck the policy-makers in Militant and it is their contention that:

> it is our tendency alone that has understood the loyalty that British workers instinctively have towards the Labour Party and that it is a movement of the class into it that will retransform it.
>
> Far from workers moving outside and against the Labour Party, history teaches us differently. Workers will not simply abandon their organisations ...

Indeed, the left in general has been gratified both by the success and by the failure of the National Front: not only does the left need the right politically, but also the progress of the Front has demonstrated both that the British 'lower' classes are not entirely unamenable to extremist politics on the one hand, and on the other, that they do not express that latent sympathy electorally. So far as Militant Tendency is concerned, these 'anti-system' politics are to be developed elsewhere:

> Genuine rank and file bodies will inevitably develop. Conferences, demonstrations, campaigns and strikes will be called by them. Marxists must intervene in these and where necessary call for such action.

The Communist Party has some 25,000 members but that figure is consistently declining; the Socialist Workers' Party, the second largest far-left group, has as little as 4,600 members, Militant Tendency about 2000 'subscribers', the International Marxist Group as few as 800. While the Communist Party in France generally achieves some 20% of the vote, and in Italy about 30%, in Britain it has never surpassed 0.4% and in the last three elections has averaged 0.1%. Despite this inconsiderable electoral impact, some of the groups on the left have taken encouragement in the decline in popular respect for the two-party system, and particularly in the decline of Labour Party fortunes. The International Marxist Group sponsored a Socialist Unity campaign in the late 1970s; the International Socialists transformed itself into the Socialist Workers' Party and, like the Workers Revolutionary Party, entered the electoral lists. Some observers estimate that the next General Election will see as many as 150 Marxist candidates standing for Parliament. But the clear signs are that Socialist Unity is foundering on the traditionally divisive preoccupations of leftist 'sectionism'. The weakness for polemical piety and partiality obviously militates against a realistically solid and enduring 'Broad Left' approach; by the same token the strategy of most appeal and most profit necessarily remains the entrist tactic. Quite simply entrism is the manoeuvre by which a group infiltrates a larger, less radical party, trade union, or pressure group, with a view to three basic objectives:

1. To identify support for its own cause within the host group, or to stimulate it;
2. To provoke and/or exploit division within that group to its own political ends and in order to achieve a degree of executive power;
3. To exert influence on the nature and direction of policy within the infiltrated group.

Entrist groups in British politics have largely been those which subscribe to the Trotskyist refinement of basic Marxism. Ideological camp in-fighting and schism has been a determining factor, for entrism is not only a political manoeuvre, it is also a refuge. When the *Tribune* journal analysed the Trotskyist movement (22 July 1977), it noted that 'the splits have come about as a substitute for action' and concluded:

> When there is no engagement in real-life political struggle and conflict, political activity must be reduced to propagandising the ideology drawn from the Marxist texts – and doing so as if it were holy writ. Because the ideology cannot be wrong, it cannot be critically examined; political activity becomes merely conflicts between different interpretations of the ideology ... So this group attacks that one, another group expels part of its membership, the infighting becomes an end in itself, the substitute for real political activity.

Entrism is therefore an attractive refuge for those groups which would not otherwise be able to sustain any real political activity. As Peter Shipley asserts in his *Conflict Study* paper on *Trotskyism: Entryism and Permanent Revolution:*

THE FOURTH INTERNATIONAL

1938

Workers'
International
League

Revolutionary
Socialist
League

1947

Revolutionary
Communist
Party

The Club

Revolutionary
Communist
Party

Socialist
Labour
League

Revolutionary
Socialist
League

Socialist
Review
Group

Young
Socialists

Posadists
1965

Young
Guards

Revolutionary
Marxist
Tendency

International
Socialists

1969
Workers'
Revolutionary
Party

Internat.
Marxist
Group

Socialist
Workers'
Party
1976

Militant
Tendency/
Labour
Party YS

Chartists

Rev.
Marxist
Current

League
for
Socialist
Action

Workers'
Fight

Revolutionary
Communist
Group

Workers'
Socialist
League

Rev.
Comm.
Tend.

Internat.
Communist
League

Marxist
Worker

Workers
League

Workers'
Power

1980

The Genealogy of British Trotskyism

> Entryism is basically a solution to the problem created by the weakness of Trotskyism and its lack of direct appeal for the working class. When the social and political climate has been distinctly unfavourable to the growth of a mass revolutionary movement ... then the tiny Trotskyist cells have sought refuge in the Labour Party ... Alternatively it has been adopted by Trotskyists when they have expected a crisis of capitalism to arise before they would have been able to prepare their own party to meet it.

Since Shipley made this evaluation of the function of the entrist tactic, revelations of Militant's activities have added a new and more assertive dimension to the practice of infiltration. But Shipley makes a crucial point with reference to the apparently humiliating lack of success that has met Trotskyist parties, particularly the Workers Revolutionary Party, at the polls:

> (The Trotskyist) does not seek a body of hundreds of thousands of people agreed on a programme that is the lowest common denominator; rather he wants a tightly built organisation of dedicated professional revolutionaries who can carry out all the tasks of propaganda and agitation that form the groundwork of Leninist revolution. This movement does not wish to succeed as a participant in parliamentary democracy but to have the capacity and the trained personnel able to turn any expressions of unrest or discontent towards revolutionary ends, and to exploit the freedoms that democracy offers. Thus entering the electoral arena is principally a propaganda exercise to spread the message, not a serious attempt to win representation in parliament.

The primary commitment of a Trotskyist faction is due entirely to that faction's interpretation of Trotsky's Marxism, his theory of the 'Permanent Revolution'. The rest is strategy.

Trotskyists believe, as Trotsky himself wrote in *The Third International after Lenin*, that 'the international capitalist system has already spent itself and is no longer capable of progress as a whole.' As that system decays, so power devolves increasingly to the masses to the point of revolutionary imminence when, according to Ernest Mandel (in *What is Trotskyism?*), 'the tension of the class relations is at its maximum and the class conflict is sharpest.' This revolutionary situation is arrived at, or so Trotskyists believe, according to strictly objective processes, in Mandel's words, 'independent of the will and control of any group or party.'

But while denying any autonomous role to political organisations or institutions, Trotsky depicted a 'subjective' element in the historical process as represented by the 'guiding layers' of the revolutionary masses, those whom he described in his *History of the*

Russian Revolution, as 'capable of making revolutionary inferences from what they observed and communicating them to others.' It was this proletarian leadership which was able to read the mystery of historical events and 'determine the moment for a blow at the enemy.' This then, is the mantle that today's Trotskyists would wish to assume for, as Trotsky wrote in his *Transitional Programme* the bible of contemporary Trotskyists, 'it is necessary to help the masses in the process of daily struggle to find the bridge between present demands and the socialist programme of the revolution ... unalterably leading to one final conclusion; the conquest of power by the proleteriat.'

The notion of the 'bridge' in the transitional programme is crucial; it also gives most significant substance to the fear that the presence of Trotskyist elements within British institutions is designedly destructive. For, as Mandel defines these 'transitional demands, they are 'those demands which cannot be incorporated or assimilated into the normal functioning of bourgeois society,' implying that the satisfaction of these demands can only be achieved in a transitional situation in which capitalism (and liberal democracy) is either overthrown or is induced to subvert itself entirely. Overthrow through subversion is the Trotskyist project.

Trotskyism appeals increasingly to potential supporters of the revolutionary left. In 1947 orthodox Communists outnumbered Trotskyists by 42,000 to 250. In 1970, the ratio was about 12:1; in 1980 the 15,000 Trotskyists of various factions amount to at least half the number of Communists. Not all the Trotskyist factions are entrist; those which pose the most serious threat are.

The Militant Tendency

In the *Sunday Times* (13 January 1980), Lord Underhill, who formerly as Reg Underhill had been the Labour Party's National Agent, was quoted as saying:

> I believe it is the duty of the national executive to tell the movement exactly what the Trotskyists and the Militant Tendency are all about, and to show the clear difference between democratic socialism and the Trotskyist outlook of what is a Marxist revolutionary party.

Lord Underhill was anticipating the refusal of the Labour Party

NEC to review or publish fresh disclosures of the activities of the Militant Tendency within the party. Indeed five years earlier, in 1975, Underhill had submitted to the NEC a report whose warnings had similarly been ignored:

> 'Militant' has its own printing works and is associated with 'Workers' International Review Publications' and 'Militant Irish Monthly'. The scale of the tendency's activities is such that it requires direction by more than an editorial board ... Those who support the Militant Tendency openly declare that it is Marxist and claim that all but one of the LPYS (Labour Party Young Socialists) Committee are supporters of the Militant Tendency.

These early findings were perhaps tentative and inconclusive; but recently they have been considerably extended and corroborated. At the time of Underhill's first report Militant supporters numbered some 500; now in 1980 membership has grown fourfold to 2000 and the Tendency has established and consolidated its position within the Labour Party. Militant has control of the LPYS, has a representative on the party's National Executive, is supported by the party's National Youth Officer, and has achieved a considerable and in many cases decisive influence in a number of constituency parties; as the *New Statesman* (11 January 1980) reports, a survey conducted at the 1979 Labour Party Conference reveals that 'the far-left Militant Tendency is the single largest faction among conference delegates, outstripping even the Tribunites.' It is therefore hardly surprising that Militant's internal documents should reflect both satisfaction for these achievements and optimism as to future success; 'the morale of most comrades is good and a confident mood exists within the tendency.'

> Our growth in strength and influence augurs well for the future. The basis has been laid in the trade unions, youth and immigrant community, for a rapid growth in the number of supporters ...

Of greater significance however, is the injunction to supporters, given Militant's presence in the Labour Party, that 'the responsibility is on each and every comrade to build the revolutionary party.'

The Militant Tendency has allegedly little influence within the British Trotskyist movement as a whole. It is criticised caustically as a 'reformist trend' for its commitment to 'internal intervention' in preference to the building of a mass revolutionary movement outside the political institutions of British society. Militant's call, following Labour's success at the February 1974 elections, for the new

Government to introduce 'revolutionary legislation' met with special derision from other Trotskyist groups. Militant had demanded the introduction of 'an Enabling Act immediately giving (the Labour Government) blanket powers to take over the monopolies, the banks, the insurance companies, to freeze banking and financial assets and establish a State monopoly of foreign trade.' But Militant thinking is quite clear; it rejects Trotskyist criticism and critical Trotskyists alike in its conviction that the Labour Party remains the party of the working class and of revolutionary progress:

This process is taking place before the eyes of the sects (Militant's epithet for rival Trotskyist groups) only they are too blind to see it.

Indeed, as the *Sunday Times* pointed out, Militant's capacity as a 'party within a party' has yielded it 'far more political impact than they could hope for as an extremist splinter group on their own.' This impact is, in the eyes of Ted Grant, Militant's elder statesman, only a modest beginning; he envisages 'a peaceful transformation of society through winning a Marxist majority in the trade unions and the Labour Party':

The unions and the Labour Party are absolutely invincible. Marx, Lenin and Trotsky pointed this out. Trotsky said that if the Labour Party has a Marxist leadership, capitalism wouldn't last six months.

To achieve this capitalist collapse, and in accordance with Trotsky's theory of transitional demands, Militant supporters are in 1980 calling for all and any socialist economic policies which they know cannot be tolerated by a capitalist system, not least by that of an ailing economy and a Conservative Government. But the Militant Trotskyists have no special affection for either the Labour Party or the trade unions; entrism is no more than a devise. As a Tendency 'Discussion Document' stated baldly:

We must never forget to train our cadres to the theoretical possibility of the unions as organisations being thrust aside, in a period of revolution, or prior to an insurrection, and that workers' committees or Soviets should take their place. But that is a theoretical possibility only. As Trotsky says, we do not make a fetish of any organisation.

On the other hand, the Document counsels, with reference to the 'politically dead old men and women' of the 'ossified little cliques' in the constituency Labour parties, 'we have to be scrupulously sure that we do not in any way give these gentlemen an excuse to take action against us.'

It is the ambiguity of this last injunction which forms the crux of the issue of Militant entrism. The political beliefs of the Tendency are open to a broad range of interpretation, as are its motives. On the left of the Labour Party Tony Benn views Militant's logic as 'indisputable' (*Sunday Times*, 16 December 1979) while Frank Allaun was indeed quoted in the *Militant* newspaper (10 March 1978), as being of the conviction that 'Militant will do a most valuable job if it helps to build a mass socialist movement'. On the right of the same spectrum, Paul McCormick, in his somewhat unbalanced book *Enemies of Democracy*, refers to a 'highly organised and tightly-knit body modelled on a guerilla army' which 'is a shadowy and secretive body of dedicated Trotskyist revolutionaries who are working secretly deep inside the Labour Party.'

The critical question therefore is: Is the Militant Tendency a Marxist pressure group within the Labour Party quite legitimately centred on its own newspaper, or is it rather a subversive party with its own programme illicitly secreting itself within the Labour Party, in breach of Labour constitution – as Shirley Williams put it, a group of 'termites burrowing their way to the heart of the party'?

Obviously, if Militant Tendency is entrist it will not disclose as much. The very title 'Tendency' is a Trotskyist style which suggests a status conferred on an informal group of people sympathetic to a certain set of principles which do not substantively conflict with the broader view of the parent organisation. It would seem quite clear that Militant's Trotskyist content rather outweighs any order of Labour orthodoxy; but theoretical evidence is circumstantially arguable. However, the Labour Party constitution expressly prohibits members from belonging to any unconnected organisations 'having their own Programme, Principles and Policy for distinctive and separate propaganda, or possessing branches in the Constituencies ... (or) owing allegiance to any political organisation situated abroad.' Lord Underhill claims evidence to indicate that the Militant Tendency is in breach of all these requirements. In the case of the first two he stated on BBC TV's *Newsnight* programme (31 January 1980) that 'the editorial boards are, in effect, their area committees and their national committee.' As for the third consideration, Lord Underhill has hitherto unpublished evidence that 'the Militant organisation has taken the lead in forming a new international body ... this body is in a very infantile state ... But the very fact that there could be members of the Labour Party linking up into a new international body when we are affiliated to the Socialist International is something that I should have thought everybody in the Party, everyone on the National Executive, whatever might be their view – Left, Right or Centre – will take a great deal of concern about.'

Until its demise in 1947, the Revolutionary Communist Party contained an uneasy alliance of three young men who have since become the gurus of extreme left politics in Britain: Gerry Healy now leader of the Workers' Revolutionary Party, Tony Cliff leader of the Socialist Workers' Party, and Ted Grant, leader of the Militant Tendency. The RCP finally disintegrated in 1950 and Grant led a faction into the Revolutionary Socialist League, publishing *International Socialist Review* and later *Socialist Fight* which, in 1963, became 'Militant'. The RSL had been formed in 1956 as the British section of the International Secretariat of the Fourth International. In 1957, *Workers' International Review* reported the RSL's resolution of the 'transformation of the Labour Party at ward and constituency level' and noted RSL's belief that:

> Our work in the Labour Party will require a slow, methodical and persistent agitation and propaganda around not only such immediate issues but also fundamental ideological questions.

The RSL remained the British section of the ISFI until the mid-sixties when it submerged in the interests of entrism. It is widely believed that when the RSL evaporated, it 'became' Militant. Certainly, Militant was established in 1964 at the premises of Workers' International Review Publications, at which the RSL was then still active; the period of overlap was very brief, and Militant emerged with a policy and a strategy bearing close resemblance to those of the Revolutionary Socialist League.

Militant established its first firm base at the new University of Sussex, where it soon took over the Labour Club. As Tom Forrester noted in *New Society* (10 January 1980):

> Five of the 17 people recently named as members of the 'Militant' editorial board were at Sussex University in this period. So were six of the 25 shareholders of WIR Publications Ltd, a Militant holding company incorporated in June 1973.

Militant in fact, despite its disapproval of 'studentism', sends its school student recruits lists of recommended universities: recently it recaptured control of the Labour Club at Sussex, following the enrolment of 15 Militant freshmen.

In 1970, 'Militant' supporters gained control of the National Committee of the Labour Party Young Socialists and, since 1972 when a change in the Labour Party constitution allowed a LPYS member onto the Party's National Executive Committee, Militant has always been represented on the NEC. Another Militant success occurred when Andy Bevan, formerly Chairman of the LPYS and Militant supporter, was appointed Labour Party Youth Officer; the appointment met with considerable opposition, but Bevan was confirmed in his post by the NEC.

Militant has also been most active in the Constituency Parties, and currently, Militant supporters are devoting considerable energies to the project of controlling local parties. This an ambition which, despite the small size of the Militant group, has met with considerable encouragement. The tactics of Militant supporters, in combination with the low level of commitment and the general disaffection of more moderate party members, render certain constituency parties more than vulnerable to persistent and intense Militant pressure. As Tom Forrester was told:

> Militant kill off organisations by their dogmatism and sectarianism. They are very boring, and they drone on at a meeting until people drift away.

Similar tactics are employed in the trade unions; a certain amount of opportunism is also encouraged, not only in the espousing of particular campaigns and causes, but also more dubious practice. A former Militant activist told Forrester:

> During strikes we were put on alert and sent in to make contact with the leaders, saying we were 'from the Labour Party'.

But Militant influence within the unions is growing; special pamphlets are prepared for specific unions, including the GMWU and the TGWU; a Militant sympathiser, Joe Marino, was in November 1979 elected General Secretary of the Bakers' Union, albeit on a 20% poll.

In general however, Militant's support has come from members of the public service unions and from students. So anxious is Militant to attract a working class, industrially-based constituency that, according to the student leader in Tom Forrester's report:

> ... they change their accents, so they all end up sounding the same. It's a sort of Liverpool accent with a bit of East End. But the aitches are dropped in the wrong places.

Despite the boredom and pretension that Militant seems to engender, the 1970s have been a period of significant growth for the Tendency. So much so that in the secret document circulated to active supporters, *Perspectives and Tasks 1974*, the 'editorial board' stated:

> Now that our horizon is extended, we should hold international schools involving members and contacts internationally, YS Schools also, but in addition, cadre schools under the banner of the Tendency.

The 'cadre' is a central concept in Militant organisational thinking. Recruitment techniques are elaborate and exhaustive, almost ritualistic, for it is the cadres who are to play the leading role when the inevitable revolutionary moment arrives. Likely recruits are usually chosen from the Labour Party or its Young Socialists and are designated 'contacts'; they are assigned 'qualified' Militants whose purpose it is to educate, persuade or convince the aspirant until his commitment and probity satisfies the local organising committee; he is then admitted to otherwise closed Militant meetings and seminars. Discipline is rigorous and exacting; supporters of the cause are expected to sell the newspaper and to attend up to six meetings a week. Progress is reviewed at a weekly branch meeting, special attention being paid to the number of papers sold and fresh contacts made by each comrade. A system of fines is instituted for defaulting or insufficiently active comrades. But as ex-Militant David James explained to *New Society* (10 January 1980):

> They do a good job on people. They give people a very good grounding in theory. They take an interest in you and encourage you. They get loyalty because they make people feel they have a role to play.

On the other hand:

> The end came for me when I stopped going to branch. A bloke came up one night and said I should have applied for permission to take leave of absence. They wanted to interview me. I told 'em to stuff it. Now they ignore me at union meetings and they've got the poison grapevine working against me.

Within the Tendency, preferment is a slow process, understandably. Despite Militant's recruiting of school-children, despite the sub-title of the newspaper — *The Marxist Paper for Labour and Youth* — and despite the central importance of the LPYS, Militant leaders, with the exception of Andy Bevan, are no longer young: Ted Grant is 67, Patrick Wall is 53, Ray Apps is 49, Peter Taaffe is 38.

Discipline extends to dogma; the Militant Tendency is doggedly isolationist. Until the TUC endorsed the pro-abortion issue, it was not deemed by Militant to be a 'class issue'. Militant instructed the LPYS to spurn the 'Campaign against Youth Unemployment' and to set up its own movement; similarly it considered the Anti-Nazi League 'not linked to an overall socialist programme', and participated only for the reason that 'a number of uncommitted youth attend some of the ANL events'. Instead the Tendency established ill-fated movements of its own among immigrant groups. Similarly, whereas it favours the withdrawal of British troops in Ulster, it shuns the 'Troops Out Movement'. 'In short', Patrick Wintour wrote in the *New Statesman* (18 January 1980), 'Militant does not like campaigns when they are not run by Militant.'

Militant's puritanism is thorough-going. Rock music and cannabis apparently 'dull the consciousness' of the working class; the women's movement is one of 'petty bourgeois women with a hang-up', homosexuality is of no consequence to the working class.

Even in the 1950s, the 'Grantites' enjoyed a reputation for puritanism and tedium. Frank Ward, a former colleague, remembered (*New Society* 10 January 1980):

> They were also by far the most unadventurous intellectually of all the groups. Healy was very energetic. Cliff and Co were busy working out new theories. But the Grantites were the dullest, most repetitious of any group. They were like a gramophone record.

Some thirty years later, the Militant Tendency is just as narrow and dogmatic. As David James foresaw:

> I disagreed with this elitist approach to the workers and I also had differences with them over their lack of tolerance towards people. A lot of them are book socialists, and I began to realise what living in a Militant-type society would be really like. There would be *less* freedom than there is under capitalism. There would be more dissidents in prison than there is in Soviet Russia. It would be a one-party state.

But the evaluation of the Tendency's significance in British politics at which the editor of *Tribune*, Richard Clements, has arrived seems singularly ill-informed. He advised *New Society* (10 January 1980):

> The best thing to do with Militant is to ignore them. From time immemorial, the Labour Party youth organisation has been the target for this type of entrist operation. But they are so sectarian and so boring, they will never get anywhere.

Indeed, nothing would suit Militant better than to be ignored. The secrecy which they practice already is elaborate. Internal documents are circulated only to trusted supporters, are numbered and unaddressed. Militant strategy is a closely guarded secret. To build a circumstantial case against the Tendency is not difficult; to produce hard evidence is not so easy. Grave suspicions have been raised in this account as to Militant's position vis-a-vis the Labour Party constitution: both its principles and its organisation certainly appear to be in conflict with Labour's regulations governing those aspects of membership. The fact that there are sister publications abroad — *Nuevo Claridad* in Spain, *Voorwarts* in Holland, *Vonk* in Belgium, *Offensiv* in Sweden — is suggestive of a further breach. The BBC's 'Newsnight' programme (31 January 1980) heightens this suspicion that Militant is the national British section of 'an international revolutionary working class movement', the CWI, which it assumes is the Committee of the Workers' International.

Ultimately the clue to Militant's real status lies in its financial affairs, dealt with separately in a subsequent section. The purpose of this lengthy account has been to provide an insight into the workings of an organisation which thrives, legitimately or otherwise, on ignorance and complacency.

The Chartists

The Militant Tendency is not the only group to have successfully entered the Labour Party. The Chartists were formed in 1970 by members or supporters of the International Marxist Group, the Workers' Revolutionary Party and Militant Tendency, with the object of imposing a 'revolutionary programme' on the Labour Party, as well as campaigning for trade unions in the armed forces, a new Fourth International and other more obscure issues.

Centred on their quarterly journal *Chartist International* and newspaper *Chartist* the subtitle of which is 'Labour's Revolutionary Voice', the Chartists have also been active, and to more radical a degree than Militant, in the LPYS. In 1972, they took over the Socialist Charter Group which had had the support of left-wing Labour. As Peter Shipley concludes:

> (The Chartist group) has been able to engage in a form of open entrism — admitting its Trotskyist faith while continuing in the Labour Party — in a manner that would have been unimaginable a decade earlier.

The Workers' Revolutionary Party

The Workers' Revolutionary Party, according to the *Sunday Telegraph* (5 March 1978) is often likened 'to one of those religious sects that sit on mountains waiting for the end of the (capitalist) world. So far they have been waiting for the revolution since 1938.' For much of that time, WRP has been dominated by the 66 year-old Gerry Healy, under whose guidance the party is regarded as probably the most fundamentalist of all the main Trotskyist groups. Also prominent in its leadership is Vanessa Redgrave whose activities, particularly in the actors' union Equity, have ensured that the WRP is newsworthy.

In line with the principle that electoral canvass is a profitable means of exposure, the WRP announced during the 1979 General Election campaign that it intended to field 60 candidates, thus to qualify for free broadcasting facilities. But WRP's participation in the democratic process is by no means token of any moderate or liberal regard. As Vanessa Redgrave expressed it, it is the WRP's conviction that Parliament is no more than 'a facade to hide the conspiracies taking place outside.' Taking into account the party's vigorous anti-Zionist stance, such a sentiment bears uncomfortably close resemblance to National Front ideology.

Among the election aims of the WRP were the advocacy of a 'revolutionary alternative' to unemployment, low wages, inflation, homelessness and racism. Also included was the intention of exposing the 'Labour traitors'; on the other hand however, the party recommended that 'where there is no WRP candidate vote Labour in solidarity against the Tory enemy, but without any confidence in the class collaboration of the Labour leaders.' In form, if not in substance, this last conviction is not far removed from Militant's view of the Labour leadership. Indeed, while the WRP is itself no longer an entrist group, its despite of the Labour Party is somewhat tempered by its aspiration towards effecting a swing to the left in the parliamentary party. WRP's rhetoric also corresponds in style as well as content to that of the Socialist Workers' Party; there is the same accent on 'revolutionary alternatives' to the Parliamentary process, the same attack on supra-governmental and anti-proletarian conspiracy, the same hostility to a complicit and treacherous Labour Party. Indeed these three strains are very closely woven in the Trotskyist commentary.

The WRP leader Gerry Healy had since the 1940s been a

The Workers' Revolutionary Party demonstrates its support for the Palestine Liberation Organisation, May 1978.

member of the Labour Party. In 1959 however, having recruited a number of former Communist Party members unhappy about the Soviet invasion of Hungary in 1956, he formed the Socialist Labour League. The League was soon proscribed by the Labour Party. By 1964 however Healy and his supporters in the Labour Party Young Socialists had contrived to take complete control of LPYS, as subsequently have Militant. But the Labour Party thereupon purged their youth organisation and the Socialist Labour League was obliged to establish its own Young Socialist group outside the Party.

In 1969, the SLL changed its name and tactics, emerging as the Workers' Revolutionary Party, equipped with a rigorous form of internal discipline, a rigid and dogmatic polemic and a reputation for secrecy and security. It views all other Trotskyist groups as 'reformist' or revisionist, particularly despising Militant for the former omission and the International Marxist Group for the latter. Indeed, at the height of media excitement about Militant's activities within the Labour Party, the WRP chose to mount a scathing attack in its youth paper *Young Socialist* (12 April 1980) upon the Tendency's 'fake Trotskyists' who 'are snuggling up closer to the right-wing that was witch-hunting them just two months ago, because in fact they have been working for them all the time.' In an editorial comment more revealing of the WRP's ideology than of Militant's, the paper inveighed against 'Militant's servility to the right-wing Labour leaders, and to imperialism itself' and took particular exception to the Tendency's condemnation of the Iranian Ayatollah, which according to WRP is 'exactly what the American imperialists and the CIA want'; WRP also despised the fact that Militant 'gave no support to the Republican movement in Ireland', that Militant was working to 'disarm workers and youth in the face of the Tory enemy ... Militant members said *not one word* about the anti-working class conspiracies at the top of the army and police.' But Militant's chief sin was that it had condemned the PLO as 'terrorist' and 'nationalistic'. By contrast, the WRP is positively sycophantic with regard to Yasser Arafat and Colonel Gadaffi and links between the WRP and the PLO are indeed most carefully maintained. In fact the recently conducted WRP petition 'Thatcher Must Talk to the PLO', was coordinated by the PLO and placed at its disposal. In print, Libya and the PLO are admired for their 'revolutionary leadership'; in private for their fraternal benificence.

The WRP's distinctly puritanical fanaticism has been the cause of several splits and purges within the party, notably when, in 1974, a faction of about 200 members broke away to form the entrist Workers' Socialist League under Alan Thornett, since anathametised as a 'guru-led' revisionist clique. The party's technique with its own defaulting members has also aroused the sort of interest more often associated with one of more obscure religious sects.

In order to broaden its appeal beyond the rigidy of its dogmatic observance, WRP has established an All Trade Union Alliance movement through which it promotes its activities in industry.

Estimates vary as to the size of WRP's membership; however, it has no more than 3000 members in the party proper, with perhaps as many as 5000 in its student-based satellite Young Socialists. Given the size of the party, and the slender means which such numbers would normally afford, it is more than merely surprising to note that apart from its journals *Fourth International* and *Labour Review*, the Workers' Revolutionary Party produces a daily paper *Newsline*, a sixteen-page tabloid with regular colour features. It is indeed remarkable that WRP is the only group left of centre, with the exception of the considerably larger Communist Party but including the Labour Party itself, that is financially able to produce a daily newspaper. Quite how WRP manages this feat will be discussed in a later section.

The International Marxist Group

When the International Marxist Group's leader Tariq Ali produced a tape-recording of industrialist Sir Richard Dobson's 'bribing wogs' speech, the IMG achieved a publicity coup of considerable proportions. Until that time, the IMG had been slowly subsiding from the eminence of the student-power era of the late 1960s and early 1970s.

The Group, held in particularly low regard by the WRP for its up-dating redefinitions of basic Trotskyism and for its ecumenical attitudes, is small in numbers, with a membership of no more than a thousand, about a third of whom are university-based. Nevertheless, the IMG, which is the British section of the United Secretariat of the Fourth International, can claim a broad influence on the far left for among its leading members are to be found prominent Trotskyist theoreticians Tariq Ali, Robin Blackburn and Ernest Mandel.

IMG was formed in 1965 around the journal *The Week* which

had been sponsored by some twenty Labour MPs, trade unionists and academics. As with the WRP, its earliest membership was derived from former Communist Party members who had resigned in 1956. For three years it followed an entrist strategy within the Labour Party but, encouraged by the emergence of the student movement of the late 1960's, publicly disclosed its Trotskyist allegiances. The Institute for Workers' Control, an organisation established partly by IMG during its entrist phase, has stayed within the orbit of the Labour Party and enjoys the support of a dozen or so MPs.

The IMG meanwhile, was prominent in the Vietnam Solidarity Campaign and has been active in other popular campaigns supportive of Castro's Cuba, Libya's Gaddafi, Troops Out of Ulster, anti-racism, anti-spending cuts, pro-abortion lobby, pro-Patriotic Front in Rhodesia.

Towards the end of the 1970s, the IMG's publications *Black Dwarf* and *Red Mole* reached a wide readership on the left; currently the Group's *Socialist Challenge* sells about 8000 copies weekly.

Despite the fact that the IMG is certainly more tolerant both of the positions of other groups and of internal criticism and variety than any other of the leading Trotskyist groups, it maintains close control over its members. The draft constitution of the IMG, agreed by its National Committee in March 1978, stresses its 'right and obligation to insist that its militants should work to implement the revolutionary Marxist programme in all spheres – "private" as well as "public".' At the 1978 Conference, it was also proposed that IMG members be obliged to attend organisational and educational meetings 'on a regular and disciplined basis' and when requested should be prepared to render an account of 'her or his area of work, theoretical reading, and the results of contact work.' It was even suggested that members intending to change residence or work should be guided by the Group as to which area they might most usefully remove.

Like the Militant Tendency, IMG sets great store by the selling of the newspaper *Socialist Challenge*; as with the Tendency, it accepts recruits into the main body of the organisation only after a vetting period of six months.

Like Militant, the IMG also recognises the importance of the Labour Party; in *The Fight for a Socialist Alternative*, its attitude is expressed:

The workers see (the Labour Party) as the only mass alternative to the Tory Party. We can attempt to change this position, but we should not attempt to deny that it exists, however subjectively painful and irksome it might appear.

This recognition of the strength of the 'reformist' appeal of Labour to the masses leads the IMG to conclude that 'left social democracy and its ideas (have) to be encountered before they (can) be combated and defeated.' The IMG therefore eschews isolationist political activity and through its sponsorship of the Socialist Campaign has aimed instead to confront reformism directly with the more radical alternative. Electoral success, it believes, will not only encourage the left in general but will in effect provoke the long-dreamed of split in the Labour Party which heralds the revolution. The campaign for the 'class struggle left wing', or 'united socialist opposition' or 'broad-based class-struggle tendency' as it is variously titled has attracted the support of a number of groups and individuals on the left, including Big Flame and other groups of former Socialist Workers' Party members. Also the readership of the IMG 'house' paper has doubled. Interestingly, in the Ladywood bye-election of 1977, the first occasion on which a candidate stood under the Socialist Unity banner, 3.4% of the poll was won, four times greater than the share gained by the SWP candidate. In contrast, the IMG candidate at Stechford had achieved only a 1.4% share in the previous spring.

The IMG is not alone in seeking to present a broad left front. The Workers' League, with a tiny membership of 120, has also committed itself to that cause; its paper *Socialist Voice* calls for the 'building of a revolutionary socialist workers' organisation in Britain' on non-sectarian principles.

But after initially encouraging signs, the cause has failed to overcome the reluctance of groups such as the SWP to join any alliance – though surprisingly SWP did consider the proposition – and has been further weakened by the general cooling of enthusiasm on the part of Big Flame and other groups.

Indeed, encouraged by recent developments within the Labour Party, IMG began in late 1979 openly debating the readoption of an entrist strategy. As the IMG is a section of the Fourth International, there could be no doubt at all as to the illegitimacy of such a manoeuvre. But if Socialist Unity is to become the mass and electoral force for which the IMG designed it, it will have to override one of the most distinctive features of far left politics, sectarianism.

There are of course other smaller Trotskyist groups whose histories are complex and confused. The International Communist League for instance, began life in the mid-1960s as Workers' Fight and in 1968, while maintaining separate identity, joined forces with the International Socialists which later became the Socialist Workers' Party. In 1971 however, the group was expelled by the IS and in 1975 merged with Workers' Power which had also been expelled by the IS, thus forming the International Communist League. But only a year later, in 1976, elements of the Workers' Power group broke away again, leaving ICL with a membership of between 100 and 150 under the leadership of S. Matgamna, and a monthly magazine *International Communist*.

Not to be confused with the Workers' Revolutionary Party, is the Revolutionary Workers' Party, a Trotskyist group of the Posadist school. The RWP is about 500 strong and pro-Chinese, producing its own *Red Flag* newspaper.

The International Spartacist Tendency, which produces *Socialist Current*, and the Spartacist League each have a membership not in excess of one hundred. The Spartacist League broke away from Alan Thornett's Workers' Socialist League in the spring of 1978 — the WSL itself having been expelled for 'dissent' from the WRP in 1974. The limited size of Trotskyist groups is however adequately compensated by the depth of commitment and intensity of rhetoric; the weakness of the left in general is almost to be measured in the dogmatic strength of resolve in the particular group. So narrow and so politically pious is the observance of each league, faction or tendency as to render them completely unself-conscious of their positions relative to the revolutionary movement as a possibility, or indeed to political life in its broadest aspects. Thus it is that the Spartacist League, reflecting upon its split with the Workers' Socialist League, proclaimed in its monthly paper *Spartacist Britain* that WSL ideology was a 'parody of Trotskyism' and stated:

> The counterposition of the Bolshevik positions of the Trotskyist Faction to the hardened right-centrism of the central leadership has brought forth another shameless defence of the majority's Pabloite attachment to the Labour Party, their capitulationist attitude to nationalism ... their all pervading economism and minimalism, and their parochialism ... we resign from the WSL.

Indeed both the strategy of entrism and the impulse towards some order of Socialist Unity can be understood against this background of ideological and political isolationism, for in their distinct and separate ways, both are efforts designed to build a real political mechanism out of the jumble and junk of the extreme left's scrapyard. The failure to date of the International Marxist Group's initiative towards a broad revolutionary movement considerably strengthens the argument for entrism as the only viable alternative available to those groups aspiring to real political influence in Britain. As has been mentioned, the lesson is not lost on the IMG itself and it can be no surprise that its leadership should consider resumption of the entrist strategy so soon after the apparent dashing of its broad front hopes. Indeed it may well be the mark of a political maturity that such groups prefer the exercise of political power to the purity and self-righteousness of particularism and 'ideological integrity'.

The political theory that Maurice Ludmer finds lacking on the right of the extremist spectrum is not by any means so under-developed on the left; indeed many observers would claim that political theory is all that exists on the revolutionary left. But the increasingly successful efforts on that wing both at entrism and in recruiting are evidence of a new and forceful element of pragmatism which informs and enforces the ideology of the larger groups; this new pragmatism is the distillation not only of political ambition, but more significantly, of a new-found, and more strongly founded, confidence in the possibility of the 'revolutionary alternative'.

The far left, like the right, pins considerable hopes on a renewed onslaught in the 1980s of the economic difficulties which so encouraged extremists in the previous decade. The left feels, with reason, that the right can no longer lay exclusive claim to the support of the 'street-fighters' of the inner city and that intellectually its own 'catchment area' is the broader. This is an analysis not entirely unplumbed by the 'popular' right but the right's ambition to restyle its image and to equip itself with a more cogent and inclusive world-view cannot be immediately realisable. Meanwhile the left has developed the organisational capacity and joint appeal to action and intellect for which the right is striving. To this extent recruitment is a street-battle between forces responding to the same impulse and in reaction to the same malaise. But the street-battle is also largely 'self-referring'; except as a form of social expression, it has little to do with real issues in the broader social context; it is thus a curiously ritualistic form of extremist self-perpetuation. It is in this light that the comment of the *Sunday Telegraph* (5 March 1978) is especially noteworthy:

> If the theoreticians on both sides were honest, they would admit that at this stage in their political journey they need each other.

Nowhere has this criticism been more firmly established than in the success of the Socialist Workers' Party through the agency of the grass-roots and street-level Anti-Nazi League.

The Socialist Workers' Party

The Militant Tendency, naturally enough, despises the Socialist Workers' Party, especially for 'ignoring the mass labour organisation and trying to find a short easy path to build a mass revolutionary party.' It is precisely SWP's pragmatic successes – so different in nature from those of Militant – to which the Tendency objects. In Militant's 1978 Bulletin, the Tendency seems to recognise, perhaps somewhat jealously, the advances which SWP had recently been making. The Bulletin levelled a jaundiced attack on SWP's weekly *Socialist Worker*, for which the party claims a circulation of 30,000, equivalent to that of the Communist daily *Morning Star* – a claim which makes Militant's criticism all the more understandable:

> (*Socialist Worker*) a paper without theory will not hold a proletarian readership for long. It will become a bore and not be of interest to the activists in the class.

It is interesting to note in this connection, that the Workers' Revolutionary Party's daily *Newsline*, in order no doubt to hold its 'proletarian readership', has introduced occasional colour features, and contains a well-informed and fairly extensive sports section.

There is considerable confusion as to SWP's ideological status; despite its early links with Trotskyism, SWP is not a member of any international socialist organisation of any official composition. Indeed the party prefers to be known as a Leninist party and while close to a number of Trotskyist positions, is politically a rather unique and self-determining group.

The seeds of the SWP were sown in the fertile ground of the mid and late 1940s when Gerry Healy, Ted Grant and Tony Cliff as young men shared in an uneasy alliance of the revolutionary left. In

1944 the Trotskyist Workers' International League and the Revolutionary Socialist League, then British section of the Fourth International, merged to form the Revolutionary Communist Party. In 1947 Gerry Healy submerged a small section of the RCP in the Labour Party and, in 1949, the remainder of the RCP followed. Thenceforward, the RCP, as an entrist operation, restyled itself informally as the 'Group' or the 'Club'. In 1951 however, a section focused on the journal *Socialist Review* was expelled from the Club over its refusal to follow the orthodox Trotskyist line which, while deploring 'Stalinism', yet supported the essentially workers' state of the Soviet Union. The Socialist Review Group reformed itself in 1962 into the International Socialists, setting its aim as the mobilisation of working class militancy. As it grew in size so the IS disengaged itself from its entrist strategy in the Labour Party. In the mid-1960s it briefly competed with the International Marxist Group for the favours of the radicalised students; but its real power base has been on the shop floor, whence it has emerged as the leading group of the militant left. To signal its transformation from pressure group status to that of a fully-fledged political party, IS changed its name in late 1976 to the Socialist Workers' Party, and began to develop a policy of 'electoral interventionism'. However its share of the poll seldom exceeded 1% and despite rising unemployment and industrial strife in the mid and late 1970s, the SWP failed to galvanise militancy to any significant degree. However, while harbouring the ambition of nominating sufficient electoral candidates to qualify for free broadcast time on the media, the SWP has reverted to a standard Trotskyist ploy: that of striking a position yet further left and leading campaigns of militant potential in the fields of unemployment (the Right to Work campaign), and racism (the Anti Nazi League). The strategy has met with considerable success; since 1976, the SWP has expanded its membership by 50% to around 5000, consolidating its main appeal in the industrial Midlands. Indeed, so forceful an impact has SWP agitation had in certain spheres – the Grunwick dispute and the anti-National Front riots at Lewisham being cases in point – that in more conservative quarters the party has gained a reputation as a movement of 'Red Fascists'. Certainly SWP's tactics derive from the Trotskyist idea of 'permanent revolution' giving rise to the public demonstration of provocative confrontation, whether with the extreme right or with the state itself. Provocation is not necessarily a spontaneous or occasional tactic; it is rather a broad and developed strategy which, as shall be illustrated later, extends beyond physical confrontation into the kind of inflammatory rhetoric in which the SWP specialises.

Among prominent SWP members are to be found Paul Foot, nephew of Michael Foot, David Widgery, author of *The Left in Britain*, Duncan Hallas, Chris Harman and Mike Kidron, South African owner of the Pluto Press, the radical publisher responsible for the production of SWP's considerable output of literature. The party however, has been dominated since its various inceptions by Tony Cliff, an Israeli who came to Britain as Ygael Gluckstein. The Party is directed by its Central Committee, elected at the Annual National Conference. The Party Council, comprised of regional representatives, acts in a consultative capacity on policy matters, as does the National Advisory Committee representing the various areas of the party's political interests and campaigns.

Unlike the IMG, which regards itself as a 'current', SWP demands a stricter orthodoxy from its members and stresses its capacity as that of a fully constituted revolutionary party. There have therefore been the predictable number of defections and expulsions throughout its history. In 1971 the Workers' Fight broke away and established itself in Manchester; in 1973 the Revolutionary Communist Group set up in Bristol with 100 members and a paper called *Revolutionary Communist*; in 1975, Workers' Power and the Workers' League which produces *Workers' Vanguard* and *Socialist Voice*, split away, as did the Liverpool-based Big Flame, similarly of 100 members, and active at Ford's Dagenham plant.

The SWP launches its main efforts in the industrial sector and has an elaborate organisational system in the factories and unions. But this is by no means an exclusive area of interest. Apart from its actual membership, of which each individual pays a monthly subscription of not less than £3, the SWP has also an affiliated 'Rank and File' movement, consisting largely of those sympathetic but not necessarily committed to the 'classic Marxist' position of the party. It has made strenuous efforts in the immigrant communities. It has a section for blacks named 'Flame' equipped with a publication of the same name; there is also an Asian group named 'Chingari' which distributes papers in Bengali, Punjabi and Gujerati; there is also a publication for the Irish minority, *Irish Worker*. Besides these, the SWP also produces its weekly paper, a journal *International Socialism* and a number of 'special interest' papers – eg for women – and pamphlets. Clearly, the party needs a sizeable full-time staff; its governing committee of ten is full-time; its offices and modern presses in East London are considerable; SWP is a large operation.

Like Militant and the IMG, the Socialist Workers' Party acknowledges the Labour Party as a working class institution, despite 'workers' illusions in Labour reformism.' But in the April 1974 edition of *International Socialism*, it was detected that working class loyalty to the Labour Party 'is residual, continuing to exist because they do not see an alternative.' The SWP clearly believes that it represents that alternative and, unlike the IMG for instance, is confident that it can detach significant areas of traditional Labour support. Hence its abandonment of the entrist strategy. With regard to this analysis, Roger Kline suggested in *Can Socialism Come Through Parliament?* :

> ... it is extremely unlikely, though not impossible, that socialists could capture control of the Labour Party. But to put one's energies into doing so is a complete waste of time. The only time the Labour Party could be captured would be at a time of massive struggles when it would be irrelevant.

SWP's task is therefore well-defined. In the edition of *International Socialism* already quoted, it was recognised that 'workers do not yet have faith in their own ability to transform society by collective action ... the job is to build up faith in collective action.' SWP believes – and it is not alone in its conviction – that political 'struggle' has during the last decade shifted considerably from parliament to the industrial arena. For this reason above all then, as Steve Jeffreys wrote in *International Socialism* (March 1975), 'the industrial struggle (is) the main field of political activity'. The 'collective action' which members of the Socialist Workers' Party have struggled to inspire in the workers has led to bitter condemnation from Trade Union leaders who are well aware of the political motives behind what Kenneth Thomas, General Secretary of the Civil and Public Services Association, describes as the 'calculated and callous exploitation of a trade union issue by a small faction.' In a circular delivered to his 240,000 members in August 1980, Mr Thomas referred specifically to the provocative involvement of SWP activists, many of whom were not CPSA members, in the picketting of the Brixton unemployment office which led to 18 arrests:

On this occasion there was absolutely no justification for prolonged and bitter unofficial action. It split the union; it could have endangered our objectives and was subsequently exploited by some whose trade unionism is suborned by their political aims.

Not only, according to Mr Thomas, had the activists 'bamboozled money out of our members and branches, trading cheaply on trade-union loyalty' but the SWP had all but completely taken control of the Brixton dispute and had exploited it for their own exclusive aims. It is clear from Mr Thomas' protest that the classical tactic of 'interventionism' – the provocation or exploitation of minor industrial grievances for political gain – has become more than an isolated feature of union affairs:

> ... There is within this union the dafter end of the political spectrum whom we have tolerated, initially with amusement, but in recent years because of our toleration they have increasingly and totally unrepresentatively misused the machinery of this union as a result of which our name has sometimes been a joke in the trade union movement.

It is hardly surprising in view of the SWP's notion of 'confrontational politics' that, like the WRP, it sees electoral participation as merely a means by which to advance its political message and not as a specifically political involvement. However, with regard to its isolationist stance it is rather more curious to note the party's flirtation with the Socialist Unity campaign and with the idea of collaboration with the Communist Party of Great Britain. Participation in the former alliance is increasingly unlikely and the SWP's reticence probably will kill off the project. Unsurprisingly, it was the SWP's unwillingness to play any but the leading role in any such movement that jeopardised the campaign. But it is almost amazing to note that a statement adopted by the Central Committee in November 1977, entitled *The Next Six to Nine Months* acknowledges 'negative features' within the SWP, namely, 'a growth of triumphalism and organisation sectarianism, a contempt among sections of the cadre for the non-SWP left.'

Any compact with the Communist Party would be problematic. There are clearly crucial policy and ideological differences and, ultimately, it is hard to see what the Communist Party with a 25,000 strong membership would gain from an alliance with the significantly smaller and very much more militant SWP. Nevertheless the strains of pragmatic 'moderatism' are interesting to note.

Altogether less moderate is the SWP's published rhetoric. The corner-stone of the party's strategy has been discussed: provocative confrontationalism has brought its rewards to the SWP, not only in the industrial arena and in the minority groups but also increasingly amongst the less expectedly politicised sectors of society. The *Sunday Telegraph* reported (9 March 1980) that the SWP's youth organisation Red Rebel had sponsored a two-day teach-in at the Polytechnic of Central London on 'revolution, socialism and the efficiency of terrorism' for 100 members of the National Union of School Students, whose National Chairman Hardy Desai, distributing a leaflet entitled 'How to Disrupt Your School in Six Easy Lessons', lectured on organising school strikes and undermining teachers' authority. But SWP's leaders were also on hand:

> The lessons started with John Deeson, secretary of the Right to Work Campaign, on why one must be a socialist. This was followed by Simon Turner, national committee member of the Socialist Workers party on terrorism. Tony Cliff, one of the founders of the party on revolution, and Maggie Wren, editor of *Women's Voice* who gave a talk, 'We Want More Sex', on sexual politics, the right to be gay and women's liberation.

In fact, this seminar is no real departure for the SWP for the party's active subversion and undermining of established authority is crucial to its concept of the struggle for 'self-emancipation'. SWP propaganda persistently seeks further to associate the organs and institutions of the state with those elements of which the state itself dissaproves or cannot condone; for instance, the fascism of the far right. In particular, the police are a prime target for such attacks, both physical and rhetorical. Typically, an SWP pamphlet (*The Fight against Fascism and For Socialism*), in describing the events following the death of Kevin Gately at the so-called 'Battle of Red Lion Square', states:

> Some demonstrators carried placards nailing Kevin's murderers – the police and the National Front ...

The article goes on to depict the SWP as the vanguard of the anti-racist campaign:

> It (the ANL) was the fruit of four years struggle against the nazis, four years during which socialists, revolutionary workers, black youth had fought a hard and lonely struggle.

Racism, the pamphlet insists, is the by-product of the capitalist system with which the Labour Party colludes, at the behest of the 'international speculators' – a phrase which along with passionate anti-Zionism, is apparently indispensible to extremists of all persuasions. It describes the conspiracy of the military, the Nazis, the Tories, Labour and Union leaders which aims at all costs to preserve the status quo at the expense of the workers; it calls for a union of the workers under the leadership of the SWP for 'if we build a revolutionary party we can present a real alternative to the Nazis. There is no other way of doing it.' Here are all the trademarks of extremist propaganda, confrontation, provocation, oversimplification, polarisation, false association, conspiracy theory; the conclusion is equally predictable:

> For those who want to change society there is only one way forward. To build a revolutionary organisation ... Revolutionary socialism does not mean building the barricades tomorrow, still less does it mean setting off bombs, or hi-jacking airplanes.
> It means being among the workers in the factories, in the mines, in the offices, in the housing estates, in the schools, fighting alongside them, supporting and encouraging the hundreds of small struggles against the effects of the present system ...
> ... Those battles will take place whether or not there is a revolutionary party. But without such a party, there won't be a network of people inside each factory, office and school, supporting each other and helping each other to win. And once defeated workers will turn on one another ... Then the concentration camps will light up with the flames of the gas ovens.

The style is typical; it is an amalgam of Sunday-school moral-teaching and barely supressed political dogma, simplistic and extravagantly general with a two-fold message: first that, the revolution is inevitable and imminent and secondly, that it is the obligation of the SWP to form the leadership in the struggle. Essentially it is elitest and apocalyptical, the two main elements of far right rhetoric. Like the right, the left including the SWP, know well what is wrong in contemporary society; they know also how to exploit these problems. Their remedies are more obscure, though dramatic. Tom Forrester wrote in *New Society* (10 January 1980) on Militant's reluctance to describe its new world, but his strictures apply equally to most of the left groups:

> Very rarely do Militant get round to discussing the type of society they favour, still less do they go into detail. ... the theoretical *Militant International Review* is typical when it simply states that Militant stands for

the replacement of 'capitalist anarchy and barbarism' with 'a harmonious, socialist, planned economy.

Except for a brief and inglorious attempt at power-sharing in Sri Lanka, Trotskyist parties have so far never tasted real governmental power. But throughout the world the various and several tiny sects through the intensity and commitment of their activities are a constant source of intrigue and irritation, not to mention disruption and at times violence. But it is in Britain that the Trotskyist torch has most effectively been kept alight and slowly but significantly these more militant and vigorous activist 'sects' are encroaching on what traditionally has been the domain of the Communist Party. It is not difficult to see why this drift towards the Trotskyist cause is taking place; the Trotskyist groups have not been slow to exploit the developing social and economic crises in capitalist society and to offer to student idealists and working class militants alike both an intellectual and an active role in the revolutionary remedy. By contrast, the Communist Party is made to seem monolithically institutionalised and bureaucratic, an impotent and bankrupt 'shadow' establishment. But, whether geriatric and moribund or not, the Communist Party remains the primary proletarian party beyond the Labour Party and is by far the largest of the revolutionary parties. In terms of percentage figures, the decline in the Party's membership and the advance on the part of the 'sects' is indeed staggering in comparison; but the actual numbers involved indicate that in terms of popular support, if not in terms of actual political influence, the threat to the Communist Party by the Trotskyists is more of a potential than an actuality.

The Communist Party of Great Britain

From a peak of 56,000 in 1942, Communist Party membership has since declined to about 25,000; similarly, circulation of the Party's daily newspaper has fallen from the 1947 peak of 122,000 achieved by the *Daily Worker* to the current figure of 36,000 held by its successor the *Morning Star*. Electoral support has also dramatically diminished; in 1945, the average number of votes won by a Communist Party candidate amounted to 4894; by 1979, the figure had sunk to 419. Quite clearly these statistics are significant evidence of the declining fortunes of the CP. But whether or not they reflect the actual picture is more doubtful. Like the Roman Catholic church, the Communist Party in times of crisis can call upon the allegiance of lapsed loyalties. In his book *Enemies of Democracy*, Paul McCormick estimates that given such an upswing, the Communist Party might well raise its membership by 100%, to 50,000, purely through the re-enlistment of lapsed members and the initiative of long-standing sympathisers. In warning against any underestimation of the CP's influence and regenerative capacities, McCormick emphasises that 'though apparently it is like a pet tiger':

> In terms of organisation, discipline, patience, long-term motivation, funds, size, and political know-how the Communist Party outclasses all other groups.

Two years after the Russian Revolution, the Bolsheviks convened the Third International, the 'Comintern', which, in stressing the necessity for 'subordinating the interests of the movement in each country to the common interest of the international revolution', was designed to coordinate the international struggle for socialism. Consequently in 1920, a number of small left-wing groups in Britain merged to form the Communist Party of Great Britain. The new organisation applied for affiliation to the Labour Party but was denied. But in 1922, a Communist was elected in the General Election on a Labour ticket. In reaction, the Labour Party prohibited CP members from Labour Party election nomination and, in 1925, excluded them from constituency branches. Nevertheless, as the only working class left-wing alternative party, the CP expanded its membership progressively over the ensuing twenty years.

In 1943, Stalin dissolved the Comintern and the European Communist Parties reverted to a concentration of interests on national means towards socialism. The CPGB embodied this focus in the *British Road to Socialism*, a document implemented in 1951 which until its modification in 1977, remained the fundamental brief of the party.

Communist Party organisation is painstaking and disciplined. The Party divides its executive functions between an Executive Committee which is elected at the bi-annual Party Congress, and a Political Committee which at its weekly meetings is responsible for the implementation of Executive Committee decisions arrived at at the EC's two-monthly meetings.

Whereas the conventional political parties organise their branches largely on a geographical basis – the Labour Party generally avoids encroachment in industrial representation which is seen as the role and function of the trade unions – the CPGB makes three distinctions at branch level, between the geographic, student and factory. Greatest emphasis is placed upon the last of these areas for it is the Communist Party's principle that:

> ... wherever possible it is desirable that our members should be organised in branches in their particular place of work. The factories are at the centre of the class struggle. Our party is seriously concerned to increase the number of factory branches and the proportion of the membership organised in this way. (*The Role of the Communist Party Branches in the Struggle for Socialism* – London 1974.)

It is therefore not surprising that, in accordance with this policy, the CP is particularly influential in the trade unions: the Communist Mick McGahey holds high office in the NUM; the Party has considerable representation in several other of the leading unions including ASLEF, ASTMS, AUEW, NUR and TGWU. In the AUEW postal balloting was introduced in order to increase membership participation in elections. Participation soared and the Communist influence declined accordingly. 'Broad Left' candidates have been defeated in all major union elections and no longer form the majority on the Executive Council, the National Committee, Rules Revision Conference or, importantly, the Delegation to the Labour Party Conference.

Such has been the decline of the 'Broad Left' that one of their main objectives has become the abolition of postal balloting.

Within the Party itself, dissent is not encouraged, and the forming of factions and tendencies is not tolerated. In its document 'Inner-Party Democracy', the position is clearly stated:

> A faction means the splitting of the Party, the establishment of a competing centre of political leadership, the establishment of loyalties other than party loyalty ... factions are dangerous.

Party members are expected to be active in their unions and party branches, and to sell the paper, *Morning Star* – a common obligation of far left groups to their respective publications. In general the party member is expected, according to Article 15 of the *Aims and Constitution of the Communist Party of Great Britain*: to 'improve (his) political knowledge and (his) understanding of Marxism-Leninism.' Indeed the development of political consciousness is a feature of the left in general and publications are regarded not so much as a luxury or as an 'in-house' service, but as a vital means of mass communication as compensation for general lack of publicity. The Communist Party apart from the daily *Morning Star*, (which in company with the *Financial Times* is often the only British newspaper available in the USSR) also publishes several journals including *Comment, Marxism Today, Labour Monthly* and *Labour Research* and, through the publishing house of Lawrence and Wishart, an abundance of standard Marxist-Leninist texts.

In common with the very much more militant Trotskyist groups, the CPGB recognises the importance of the Labour Party in working class politics. In the March 1977 issue of *Marxism Today*, the CPGB General Secretary, Gordon MacLennan, stated unequivocally:

> Anyone who 'writes off' the Labour Party, the party of the working class, not recognising its vital role in present and future political affairs in Britain, is making a fatal error.

MacLennan's analysis of Labour's agency is however rather more generous than that of the Trotskyists and, accordingly, CPGB thinking does not exclude the function of political dialogue-confrontation with the forces of Social Democracy. As stated in the redrafted *British Road to Socialism*, the CP:

> does not ... seek to replace the Labour Party as a federal party of the working class, but rather ... see(s) a much more influential Communist Party as crucial to the future of the Labour Party itself.

To achieve this goal, the Communist Party sets itself to strengthening the leftist impulse within the Labour Party against the reformist influence, by galvanising the trade unions and by demonstrating at the polls the popular support for socialist policies. The Labour Party will thus be drawn politically closer to the Communist positions, will relax its proscriptions so that the trade unions will be free to elect Communist delegates to the Labour Party. The resultant Labour-Communist Party alliance, it is hoped, will then be in a position to implement socialism in Britain.

In reviewing the publication of the draft version of the new *British Road to Socialism* which set out these objectives, the *Times* editorial (2 February 1977) recognised that for the Communist Party:

> ... it is a much more realistic purpose to seek the extension of the left-wing influence within the trade unions and the Labour Party. That is where the main Communist threat lies at this time, and the threat is all the greater

because it is not confined to the Communists. Indeed the different Trotskyite groups are in all probability now a greater menace ...

The *Times* writer – apparently regarding the Socialist Workers' Party as among the 'different Trotskyite groups' – recognises the comparative moderation of the CPGB. Indeed this somewhat surprising degree of 'democratic circumspection' is borne out in Peter Mair's condensation of the CP's newly modified ideological strategy:

> Socialism might be won through parliament, though a parliament with a democratised state machine (e.g. civil service, armed forces etc.); and, while government might enter into a closer, though unspecified, relationship with the Labour movement outside parliament, the ultimate authority of parliament will neither be challenged nor abridged. Nor will the right of other parties to contest elections be forbidden, even those parties hostile to socialism.

Such 'temperate revolutionism', together with the Communist Party's conciliatory attitude towards the Labour Party, contrast strikingly with that of, for instance, the SWP, whose opinion of the Labour Party and its function and whose disbelief in the possibility of democratically-inspired or institutionalist revolution render any alliance with the CP very much more improbable than appears recently to have been the case.

The *Times* editorial implied that the future revolutionary threat lies to the greater degree with the Trotskyist factions. Whether this prognosis is sound or not, it is certainly significant that while the CP declines in strength that of the SWP, the WRP, the IMG and the Militant Tendency grows apace. The relative moderation and avowed democratic observance and sobriety of the Communist Party is steadily being overhauled by the current appeal of a more esoteric Trotskyist ideology which places its emphasis on dogmatic 'objective' faith, activism, disruptive interventionism and intolerance and on unbridled militancy. The revolutionary establishment itself is under siege.

The Communist Party of Great Britain is not subject to the rifts and schisms which beset other far-left parties, or at least not to any significant degree. Since the resignations of 1956 over the Soviet intervention in Hungary, the CPGB has increasingly recognised the difficulty inherent in too close an association with the Soviet Union. More recently, the Party's drift away from the Soviet model towards the principle of Eurocommunism has however precipitated a rift of the opposite nature. In 1977, upon publication of the new draft *British Road to Socialism*, a 1000 strong splinter broke away in defiance of the prevailing trend. Hardly surprisingly, its critics denounce the *New Communist Party* as Stalinist in ideology and constitution.

The Communist Party of Britain (Marxist-Leninist)

With a complement of about 500 members, the CPB (M-L) is the largest Maoist party in Britain and, as such, has been partially recognised by the Chinese. Founded by Reg Birch, an Executive Councillor of the AUEW until his recent retirement, the CPB(M-L) through its paper *The Worker* expresses an implacable emnity to the concept of 'social democracy' and pillaries the Labour Party as an organisation having 'nothing to offer the working class except treachery'. The CPB(M-L) does not discount the use of armed guerilla struggle on behalf of the oppressed working class.

A smaller Maoist party which distributes *Workers' Daily* and specialises in industrial disruption to quite considerable an effect, is the Communist Party of England.

The Revolutionary Communist Party of Britain (Marxist-Leninist)

While seeming not altogether ill-disposed to the Albanian Communist Party and its leader Enver Hoxha, the RCPB(M-L) indulges in unbridled contempt not only for the British and American establishments, but also for those of the Soviet Union and China. It is similarly vitriolic in its detestation of the CPGB and the Trotskyists alike. Typical of its obsessive style of frantic denunciation is the reaction of its paper *Workers' Weekly* (3 November 1979) to the recent visit to Britain of the Chinese leader Hua Guofeng. Describing RCPB(M-L)'s picketting of the Sino-British 'reactionary alliance', the paper states:

> The comrades hoisted the red banner of the RCP(M-L) and placards reading 'Down with the Chinese revisionists', 'Down with the visit of Hua Guofeng to Britain', 'Down with US and British imperialism', 'Down with Soviet and Chinese social imperialism'. These were the slogans shouted loudly and militantly that met Hua Guofeng as he emerged from his celebrations under heavy police guard. Following the departure of the

revisionist chieftain, the police launched a vicious attack on the picket which met with resolute resistance and vigorous denunciation ...

Thus it is that the state in general and the police in particular are accused not only of protecting and succouring the far-right, but the extreme left as well. As the *Workers' Weekly* continues:

Thus the British imperialist state puts ... the Chinese social-imperialists under its protection and care, while it attempts to suppress the opposition of the Marxist-Leninists, of the proletariat and people of Britain.

In the belief that exposure to such blind and hateful rhetoric may be at least salutary, it is worth including one further extract from the same article. Describing the Chinese leader's visit to Karl Marx's grave at Highgate, the paper declares:

The comrades of the RCPB(M-L) organised vigorous picket to oppose this outrage, this cynical desecration of the grave of the great leader and teacher of the international proletariat by the Chinese revisionists and the British imperialists – the vicious enemies of Marxism, socialism and the world's people. Once more the Chinese revisionist leader was denounced to his face for all the crimes carried out against the Chinese people and the world's people.

Further comment is superfluous; speculation as to the nature of a society over which the RCP(M-L) would preside is unnecessary.

There are of course a myriad of other left-of-Labour groups, factions, fractions, tendencies and parties, ranging from the 800 strong Socialist Party of Great Britain founded in 1904 whose paper *The Socialist Standard* is evidence of its consistently moderate and democratic conviction, through organisations such as People's Democracy, prominent in which is Michael Farrel, which began its existence in 1968 as Socialist, progressed to Marxism in 1972, and in 1976 arrived at Leninism. Its paper *Unfree Citizen* places much emphasis on 'British imperialism' in Ireland. There is the Communist League, formed in 1967 as the Marxist-Leninist Organisation of Britain and pushing an 'anti-revisionist' line through its publications *COMbat, COMpas* and *InterCOM*; there is the Young Communist League of Great Britain formed in 1922 to educate young people in socialist theory, with a membership of some 2000 and journals *Cogito* and *Challenge*. There are besides, the League for Socialist Action, the Revolutionary Communist Tendency, the Communist Workers' Organisation which sells *The Communist*, the Communist Workers' Movement, and more.

There are also a number of independent publications (for instance *The Leveller*) and research agencies on the left, equivalent to the rightist Aims of Industry and Freedom Association. Among them are to be found the Institute for Race Relations whose journal *Race and Class* speaks for itself, State Research which monitors developments in rightist politics and rightist influences in 'state politics', the Bertrand Russell Peace Foundation and the Institute for Workers' Control which both are associated with the Labour Party.

In addition to the various Marxist groups following to their various degrees the teachings of Marx, Lenin, Trotsky, Mao and Hoxha, there is another set of leftist groups: the Anarchists, some of which have a quasi-Marxist philosophy, though most do not.

The Anarchists

Among the quasi-Marxist Anarchist groups the Libertarian Communists are most prominent. Known formerly as the Anarchist Workers' Organisation and the Organisation of Libertarian Struggle, the Libertarian Communists produce their own paper *Anarchist Worker*. Similarly Marxist inspired though with serious qualifications, the Anarchist Workers' Association was formed in 1971 as the Organisation of Revolutionary Anarchists, to promote the concept of 'self-activity' on the part of the working class towards a 'libertarian communist society'. The anarchist papers *Libertarian Struggle* and *Libertarian Communist* are particularly critical of those elements of Marxism-Leninism which they ajudge to be 'illiberal'. In the January/February issue of the latter publication, the writer stated the nature of such objection:

> However, we are not uncritical of the mainstream, Leninist revolutionary tradition in Britain. Most of the groups in this tradition have a rigid and elitist view of the nature and role of revolutionary organisation. They also seem to have at best only a paper commitment to democracy in the revolutionary process and to the control of the means of production by the working class as a whole.

But despite this trenchant critique, the anarchists, Marxist or otherwise, have exerted inconsiderable influence on political life in Britain during the last ten years and more. Marxist counter-critics see the anarchists as misguided idealists out of touch with real issues and forces which govern and determine social life and revolutionary conduct, and to a substantial extent the criticism is valid. The reluctance on the part of anarchists to concede to any form of organisation or doctrine which may be or become an 'establishment' is a considerable obstacle, if only a psychological one, to concerted or deliberate political activity. Nevertheless anarchist thought, particularly in its libertarian context, has played an important role in the concept and formulation of 'spontaneous' and community activism. As Ian Walker observed in his survey of 'Anarchy in the UK' (*New Society* November 1979):

> Over the last fifteen years, anarchist ideas and methods organisation have had an impact particularly on the 'alternative society' of lifestyle politicos, on the women's movement, in squatting and other forms of community activism, on punk.

Anarchy as a form of political expression had its hay-day during the years of the Spanish Civil War; since that time its limitations as a coherent activist movement have rather exposed it to a kind of intellectual or ideological fragmentation which could be involved in both the pacific CND movement of the 1950s and 1960s and in the somewhat less passive social protest of the Angry Brigade of the early 1970s. Indeed since the demise, or capture of the Angry Brigade, British Anarchism made no serious assault on press attention until the celebrated 'Persons Unknown' trial of 1979. Indeed, it would be appropriate criticism to depict the broad anarchist trend as one chiefly populated by either nostalgic veterans or, currently, by confused young punk-rock fans who seek specifically an uncommitted and unarticulated form of rebellion.

There are however serious, thoughtful and actively involved anarchist groups many of which centre upon publications such as *Freedom*. Another such is *Black Flag*, the organ of the 'Black Cross' established by Stuart Christie who also runs the Cienfuegos Press named after the Cuban revolutionary. Christie himself is an experienced and committed anarchist, formerly involved with the Angry Brigade and who has previously served a prison sentence for an alleged attempt on the life of General Franco in Spain, the arena of anarchism's most dramatic obduracy. *Black Flag* seeks to come to the aid of political prisoners throughout the world, with particular concentration on those in Northern Ireland. However, Christie's activities in the secluded Orkneys have recently attracted the close attention of the Special Branch which is currently investigating a manual produced by the Cienfuegos Press which, under the title of

Towards a Citizens' Militia, advises on guerilla and terrorist tactics. Published on behalf of the International Revolutionary Solidarity Movement, First of May Group, the 28-page handbook deals explicitly with such information as how to mount ambushes and strategic sabotage, how to use weapons and explosives and how to conceal them, how to deal with security personnel and how to resist interrogation techniques. Allegedly compiled with the expert advise of former members of the Provisional IRA and the Ulster Volunteer Force, the publication has, according to Christie, attracted advance orders from the Ministry of Defence, the CIA, the FBI, and from the Soviet Union and China. While the foreword to the manual denies that it is advocating the adoption of political violence so much as advising on the tactics of 'resistance' should the civil and political freedom of the 'man and woman in the street' come under attack, the manual constitutes a text-book for terrorists. The caption to one of several diagrams instructs:

> An explosive is only effective if it is closely confined, for example by packing it inside a piece of scaffold pipe, solidly capped at either end. Systematic weakening of the pipe produces a vicious fragmentation grenade.

Unsurprisingly, the *Daily Telegraph* reported (11 August 1980), that the manual is presently in the hands of the Home Secretary and the Director of Public Prosecutions.

Another veteran Nicolas Walter, editor of the *New Humanist*, is involved with *Freedom*, a journal which in the past attracted regular contributions from such notables as Herbert Read, Alex Comfort, Ethel Mannin and George Orwell. But in general the anarchist tradition is hardly sustained and the thought and example of Kropotkin, Bakunin and Malatesta tends to be submerged in the more eccentric, less reflective and certainly more frenetic rebelliousness of adolescence. While the groups like Solidarity and those mentioned above strive to bring some political application to the anarchistic impulse, the encircled A has come to represent a less elevated or principled revolt against the nature of authority. Organs such as *On Yer Bike, International Anthem, The Eclectic* and *Existencil Press* no longer command the attention or the respect of intelligent criticism.

Nevertheless, the anarchists have been active and prominently so in various lobbies, including 'Spies for Peace', CND, anti-censorship, anti-hanging and generally on behalf of minority rights, and it would be accurate to state that their influence is to be found more within these general libertarian campaigns than in concerted and exclusive action. Anarchism's central concept of revolt is indeed crucial to revolutionary theory; in practice however, its lack of controlling and cohesive doctrine renders it no serious political challenge either to the conservative or revolutionary establishment. As Ian Walker points out:

> Some of those who shop in the supermarket of ideas are attracted to anarchy, but most aren't. It does not have the respectability of Marxism ... Yet the anarchists have always had an influence, even in Britain, out of all proportion to their numbers.

Perspectives and Conclusions

The Extremist Precedent

Writing in *The Times* (18 June 1977), George Hutchinson asks:

> Democratic though we are, have we not been over-indulgent in allowing the National Front the freedom it so wantonly abuses?

The question is central to the liberal dilemma when facing the problem of political extremism in general. But liberalism as a form of political philosophy is essentially a politic of compromise; in spirit it is itself a denial and neutralisation of extremist impulses; in practice however, it necessarily eschews recourse to proscriptive self-protection. In this way, it is an imperative element of the liberal theory that tolerance should extend not only to dissenting fellow liberals, but also further, to those who would acknowledge no such mutual contract of tolerance at all, those who care nothing for democracy or for its liberal precepts. In its barest form, the belief that the liberal system stands or falls on its own merits renders any intelligent answer to Hutchinson's question impossible. Crucially, this belief freezes the liberal into political impotence for it implies that if liberalism responds to extremism, it can only do so in an illiberal manner: if under extremist seige liberalism concedes, it thereby surrenders itself to its enemy; but if it equips itself for battle, then it becomes an enemy to itself. Ironically however, this is precisely the analysis made by the extremists themselves and one which directs much of their provocative and confrontational strategy. The corner-stone of Trotskyism is the politics of the 'transitional demands', a theory which dictates the fundamental importance of forcing the democratic society into a position where it must react to the stimulus of anti-democratic forces. If, as suggested above, it concedes it has subverted itself; if on the other hand it seeks to defend itself, it must alienate itself from itself, thus provoking yet more dire conflict. In either case, it delivers itself up to the extremists.

But should the principle of tolerance be so self-subversive an inhibition? If liberalism falls into a state of disuse or decay, are we still not free to prefer it to any or all extremist alternatives?

The purpose of this paper has been to a large extent, to put before the public the nature of those alternatives from no partisan or partial motive except that of democratic liberalism itself. The hope and belief is that a better informed public is a better protected one for the strength of democracy depends almost exclusively on the ability of the individual citizen to choose, and to know and understand from what he chooses. It is the strength of conviction and of 'informed selectivity' on the part of the individual and ultimately of the broad masses of individuals which reinforce and reaffirm the liberal system. The freedom of rational choice and therefore of tolerant though decided preference is a freedom above all to preserve. As George Hutchinson so trenchantly concluded:

> To conceal the reality, to disguise the truth, intentionally or unintentionally, is to invite political – that is to say social – discord or worse.

It is crucial to realise that the extremist groups in British politics do not constitute a 'lunatic fringe', and that there is a world of difference between a 'Silly' candidate who polls 100 votes and a Workers' Revolutionary Party candidate who may poll still fewer. It has also to be recognised that election returns do not disclose the whole story by any means. Parliament may to one arguable extent or another reflect the 'will of the people', but it cannot, indeed does not, always protect that interest from the undue influence of the infiltrator, the disruptor and the street-fighter. Social indifference or complacency are the food and drink of the extremist cadres; disaffection and disillusionment are the measures of his success.

The past decade has been a difficult period for the Western democracies and not least for British society. But while certain, particularly economic, problems have been impossible to surmount in the short term, Britain's political leadership has consistently failed to grasp the social nettles which have so persistently thrust their way up through the social fabric. In consequence a political vacuum has developed in the more arid zones of the political hinterland which small but uninhibited extremists groups have not been slow to fill. Michael Meacher, Chairman of the Labour Coordinating Committee, whilst referring to the Militant Tendency's 'occupation' of the Labour Party, may well have extended his diagnosis to cover the broader political spectrum. Militant's appeal and influence, he claims, have taken root in 'the fertile ground of disillusionment with Labour governments. This problem would fade away if we had a Labour leadership which reflected the aspirations of the broad mass of the labour movement.' Yet, even now when Militant's activities within the Labour Party have been disclosed, the Party at the highest level falls into the trap of liberal impotence as described above, and contents itself with honourable but ultimately misguided and vacuus pledges to preserve a 'broad church' against 'witch-hunts', oblivious apparently of the decadence of a church in which the atheist and blasphemer kneel beside the true believer. Again, the *Observer* editorial (27 January 1980) though dealing with Militant, can usefully be broadened in scope:

> The only long-term way for sensible Labour people to combat it – and the other factions which would doubtless follow – is to build up their own membership and revive the party's democracy ... Meanwhile, Militant requires more robust opposition than it has so far received.

The extremist parties are extraordinarily reticent about the actual composition of their visionary societies and brave new worlds. But without the constraints of responsibility and accountability which act upon the major parties, the extremists are free to take a purely reactive, and implicitly exploitative, position on societal problems. Though obvious, it needs stressing that extremist groups make most rapid headway when society's concern over such issues as unemployment, inflation, immigration, crime, diminished housing, health and education services is at its most intense. The National Front (or that fragment which retains the name) is quite explicit in its recognition of such opportunities. A members' bulletin despatched in July 1980 under the title *Our Plans for the 1980s* asserts quite blandly:

> If it is true that the National Front has no hope of gaining power under conditions that are stable economically, socially and politically we should not be preoccupied with making ourselves more 'respectable' under present conditions. We must appreciate that the 'image' that we have been given by the media and which may well lose us some potential support today, will be a positive asset when the streets are beset by riots, when unemployment soars, and when inflation gets even beyond the present degree of minimal control.

Again it should be emphasised that the extremists are more content to exploit such problems than to offer constructive remedy. It is open to question if all these difficulties will be resolved in the predictable future, whether by the present Conservative Government or under a return to Labour. But even if it were possible, the extremists would not disappear for they have worked hard in what for them have been propitious times to establish their enclaves, and establish them they have. The extremists have long recognised that power without popularity is very much the securest and most dependable means to an end. Entrism is precisely that abrogation of influence which circumvents the democratic process. As a tactic of what could appropriately be described as 'guerilla politics', it is not unakin to political blackmail or ransom; by such means it is very much more realistic a proposition for the satisfaction of unreasonable demands than an appeal to popular support.

Those groups which do not practice entrism have made their presence very much felt on the streets; the Socialist Workers' Party for instance, understands that when people are forced by consideration of personal or communal security or by conscience to take sides their commitment is not always thoroughly discriminating. In this way, the Anti-Nazi League has served as a most profitable power-base for the SWP. Similarly in terms of lobby and propaganda, the National Front understands that colour-prejudice is not synonymous with fascism; but it is the thin end of the NF's rather thicker wedge. As Martin Webster admits, 'it takes quite a lot of psychological courage to put that first cross for the Front.' Other smaller groups are content to bide their time and build their bases. Some undoubtedly are insignificant, the detritus of the larger organisations. But some are not, and particularly on the ultra-right small cells without direct political ambition are providing logistic and armed support for their ideological comrades.

It is simply neither useful nor appropriate to describe the political extremes as a lunatic fringe.

Nor is it constructive necessarily to draw too firm a conclusion from the apparently inconsiderable membership strength of extreme factions. For, as indicated earlier, extremist groups have largely disencumbered themselves from the broad demands of, and necessary concessions to mass-populism in order to concentrate their considerable energies on the building and consolidation of organisational bases, independent of 'causes' and therefore free to withstand shifts in popular interest and opinion.

The optimistic vapidity of the 'Youth Movement' of the 1960s has served as a useful lesson, particularly to the left which realises that the mobilisation of the masses is by no means a spontaneous 'event'. Idealism has been overcome or supplanted by strategy, just as the libertarian and unaligned Bohemian and the hippy have been replaced by the ideologue the political puritan and the zealot. Egalitarianism having failed, the revolutionary elite has taken over the management of the 'revolutionary alternative'. As *Tribune* pointed out in July 1977:

> The revolutionary leadership is primarily concerned to influence ... and create a disciplined organisation of cadres to be thrown into action in a pre-revolutionary situation.

Tribune also underlined the strategic intentions of the Trotskyist groups in particular as being more calculated than many would allow:

> ... the existence of Trotskyist groups inside or outside the Labour Party has little to do with short-term and comparatively minor matters such as the future of right-wing MPs. It has much to do with a long-term, far-reaching strategy and method of political organisation and operation.

The factions have equipped themselves with resilient structures and resourceful strategies which render them proof against the transience of 'social phenomena' and afford them an influence and an operational capacity and potential quite out of all proportion to their numerical strength in membership.

Chaotic, dogmatic, obscure, miniscule the fringe may be; but its hardened and experienced nucleus of committed and resourceful activists is in many ways better equipped and better prepared for the 1980s than the British establishment itself.

Extremism and the Opportunity of the 1980s

As explained, the extremist groups in general have established a form of 'internal dynamic' quite exclusive and independent of the larger political world and its demands. In any economic event, boom or bust, the factions have laid their ideological strategies and there can be no reason to expect a diminution of extremist activity. Indeed quite the reverse is infinitely the surer prospect.

Extremist involvement in mainstream politics has been dealt with at length. However, recent developments have served to encourage the fringe groups still further. Not only have the major parties shown insufficient resolve to deal with their resident 'fifth columns', but renewed and serious debate over the formation of a new party of the centre represents a multiplicity of consequences which have crucial bearing on the future of moderate politics in Britain. Indeed the proposed 'third party' presents a microcosmic insight into the current vulnerable state of British politics.

If it attracted any significant level of prominence it would indicate a despair on the part of the moderates, particularly those within the Labour Party, at the increasing authority exercised by the radical wings of both major parties, and at the simultaneous and related extension of extremist influence. There is indeed a compelling irony in the conviction of Cambridge economist Bob Rowthorn when he told *The Times* (10 March 1980), that, 'the far left groups have become much weaker and the Labour left much stronger. In 1969 Tariq Ali was the main draw in publicity terms. Now it is Tony Benn.'

But this despair is crucially significant in itself, for it is in part symptomatic of a recognition, indeed expression, of the poverty and impotence of political moderation and its inability to control or restrain the efforts of the activists, or impose the will of the majority over the few. The project of a third party is thus a singularly negative impulse in conception. But further, in the event the initiative may be yet more damaging.

Critics of the putative party stress that for manifold reasons, such a party would have no real electoral constituency in the country and that in consequence its formation while being a response to the increasing polarisation of the main parties, will actually serve only to intensify and accelerate that polarisation, thus weakening the moderate cause not only in both those parties but also in the country as a whole. As a result, it is feared, the party machines will be broken down still further, rendering the parties still more accessible to the intrusion and interventionism of extremist activists, in turn confusing and debilitating the political scene yet further.

Such a scenario is clearly one which greatly encourages extremist ambitions; an amorphous and socially unrepresentative centre moderate party, offering, as Ronald Butt suggested in *The Times* (24 January 1980), no more than a regurgitation of 'old and failed ideas', buffering on the one side a hard-line right-wing Conservative Party, and on the other, a militant left-wing Labour Party – none of which would be truly acceptable to the electorate or, for that matter, to each other.

It is against this background of uncertainty, confusion and

disaffection that the extremists are motivated to operate with redoubled vigour. Confusion and irresolution afford these groups the cover they need and the justification they require for their various activities. Similarly, the lack of political leadership and conviction makes the recruitment task at 'grass-roots' level among the dissatisfied and disadvantaged all the easier for the extremists.

The political arena is crucial. If the major parties cannot or will not protect themselves and thus the nation's confidence in the democratic institutions, then there can be less hope in the other fields of contention.

Clearly union militancy is to a large degree both symptom and cause of the current lack of political, social, economic and industrial cohesion in Britain. But it is also significant to note that 'union militancy' is largely a myth. The active militants within most trade unions are in number insignificant; in influence however they may well be powerful, but this is generally only because the more moderate amongst their union colleagues are apparently indifferent to both the effectiveness and the responsibility of their union vote, secret or otherwise. The idea of 'union militancy', inextricably linked as it is to the 'silence of the majority' which having surrendered the initiative to the voluble minority is all the less inclined to regain it, is one which needs to be viewed with a great deal of circumspection. But such militancy as there is has also been stimulated by the interventionism of the extreme left and, to a lesser extent, by the intrigue of the extreme right. The left eager to provoke class confrontation, and the right equally intent on confronting the left and on provoking repressive anti-union measures from the state, can obviously be expected to involve themselves yet more intensely in trade union and shop-floor politics.

The schools also have increasingly become the target for extremist activity and recruitment, notably as practiced by the National Front and the Socialist Workers' Party. The British Movement and the Militant Tendency are now also turning their attention to this arena.

While the left concentrates its efforts on the industrial workers and on the immigrant communities, the right is moving towards the middle classes, exploiting the fear of trade union militancy not only in industry and commerce but in the armed forces as well, when possible.

Nor are the Churches sacred. The right is mobilising its effort 'For Christ and Race', under the encouragement of American 'Christian' racists:

> Yahweh says we are His Battle Ax. Let us get out the grindstone, sharpen the Ax, and get to work.

The move into such areas of involvement is one which can be expected to intensify in the 1980s, particularly if, as expected, new recessions befall the Western world. The problems already described on which the extremist parasite feeds will clearly continue to effect most critically the lower socio-economic classes; but they will begin, indeed have already begun, to erode the traditional advantages of the middle classes. The right, and in particular the National Front, is quite clearly adjusting its strategy to embrace the traditionally more stable elements in society which, it feels, will soon feel the need to turn to more extreme solutions for more extreme or uncomfortable problems. The middle class is an all but untapped reservoir. The left too, in its own way, has partially sensed that at the right moment considerable electoral advantage may be taken. The Socialist Unity campaign was to some extent evidence of its sponsors' awareness that real popular headway could be made if more attention was paid not only to unity and alliance but also to image and repute, and not only with appeal to the 'rank and file' but also to the disaffected middle class.

Whatever the social conditions which prevail throughout the present decade, extremist groups will be consolidating their bases and extending their operative and logistical apparati, probing and exploiting the vulnerabilities of the democratic society.

It is clear that in a social climate of stress and unrest, extremist groups are at their most intrusive; it is apparent also however, that in periods of comparative economic progress, they can be most dangerous. In the event of economic boom, the extremists well realise that popular support is at its lowest in potential as well as in fact. This consideration does not deflect their purpose; it merely concentrates their energies upon the more exclusive and illegitimate of their activities – ultimately, terrorism. The economic prosperity enjoyed in recent years by Japan and West Germany has been accompanied by a 'terrorist boom', an extreme expression of frustration on the one hand, and determination on the other, both motivated by an utter despite of liberal democracy and its social life.

But before we turn to the terroristic extension of extremist politics, there is yet one further aspect of the political underworld on which attention should be focused, namely finance. Whatever the intensity of commitment and the organisational capacity of the factions, ultimately they must depend upon hard cash for without it all the idealism or pragmatism in the world will not launch a cause or a campaign, a programme or a project.

The Funding of Extreme Groups

Almost all extreme groups distribute at very least one newspaper or journal, and it is very doubtful that any of these publications is, at best, anything more than self-supporting. The straightforward and formal method of financing is naturally through membership and subscription fees, but it is unlikely that, given the size of most memberships, sufficient revenue can be raised in this way to finance the full range of activities and overheads of an active organisation. So the question remains, in the words of George Hutchinson:

> Where does the money come from? ... If we could discover all the sources, and know them with certainty, we should at once understand more of the larger political reality underlying this odious movement and its odious purposes.

While Hutchinson was referring specifically to the National Front, the same question applies across the spectrum.

The parties themselves are understandably secretive about their financial sources, as they are about most of their operations. But when it is considered that the cost of a parliamentary candidate's electoral deposit is £150 and that in 1977 the National Front declared its aim of contesting all seats in the next General Election, the letter of protestation published in the *Hinkley Times* of 30 September of that year is especially ingenuous. The local NF Chairman, John Ryde, wrote:

> ... the National Front is self-financing ... We have the usual rummage sales, weekly totes etc, but in the main the money comes out of the pockets of party members and supporters with some candidates paying their own deposits. We also receive anonymous donations through the post, mostly from people ill able to afford them ... This next general election will see the bonus of saved deposits.

Mr Ryde's assertions needs must be considered with the same critical circumspection as should attend the general canon of

National Front publicity and propaganda – similarly the claim of Peter Taaffe, editor of *Militant*, that:

> All our money derives from active workers in the labour movement. We don't receive any money from sinister foreign or domestic sources.

It is certainly true that the Militant Tendency in particular is able to collect substantial amounts of money from its subscribers and supporters; it is not unusual that a meeting of only twenty individuals will yield up to £50 or £60 to the passing hat. Nevertheless, by no means could the Tendency fund its considerable organisation on such an income. Ultimately Peter Taaffe's allusion to 'sinister sources', in the absence of more convincing detail, loudly begs the question.

Finance: The National Front and the Right

In his paper on the National Front (No. 97 in the *Conflict Studies* series, July 1978), Peter Shipley advised:

> Industrialists do not finance the NF, nor does it enjoy the support of any famous or influential figures of the type who backed Mosley.

It is certainly true that the National Front has so far failed to attract solid support among the governing or monied classes; nor has it to date offered much appeal to the section of the intelligensia which found itself not ill-disposed to Mosley's fascism in the 1930s. But, as suggested earlier, the Front is beginning tentatively to broaden its constituency. It is already inaccurate to infer that the National Front has found no patrons in the business world. Indeed in 1977 the Business section of the *Observer* (5 June) revealed:

> There are suggestions that the National Front could soon be receiving its first 'political contribution' from a publically quoted company ... the mooted benefactor is one of the smaller independent breweries ...

Somewhat less ambiguous – in fact quite explicit – was the attempt made in 1978 by a group of businessmen in South Wales to raise funds for the National Front. Dated 10 December, a confidential letter from Mr R.P. Farr of the 'Fire 'n' Freezer Centre' of Port Talbot informed a local businessman:

> I have been chosen to act as spokesman for a group of local businessmen who are clubbing together to raise money for the National Front election

campaign in South Wales. Naturally some of these men prefer to remain anonymous for business reasons, whilst others do not mind coming out into the open such as myself ...
We are donating to the National Front sums of money between £10 and £150. Perhaps you would like to include some of your business associates who might be interested. I have heard tell of a businessman's club in Swansea whose members are mildly sympathetic to the National Front ...

Mr Farr's initiative, tentative though it may appear, is nevertheless most significant. While still dealing on the 'petty bourgeois' level, the Front has nevertheless enhanced its standing in the business community, at least one step up from 'corner shop' commerce. On the national scale Mr Farr's exercise raises very considerable sums of money for the Front; but such fund-raising activity is hard to sustain without a specific objective such as a general election, and will not meet the Front's ever expanding ambitions.

It is therefore of profound interest, and indeed concern, that investigations indicate that in 1977, the National Front received a most substantial offer from a group of sympathetic, or rather recreant, Conservatives which included a member of the House of Lords, formerly a considerable benefactor of the Conservative Party itself, a merchant banker and a property magnate. Conditional, in the first instance, upon the dismissal of Martin Webster and the modification of certain of the Front's parliamentary ambitions, finance was to be provided for the acquisition of a new Headquarters with club facilities, and towards the funding of a 100% expansion of the National Front's print programme within twelve months. The sum of money under consideration would have had to be in excess of at least £100,000 and it is important to note that this transaction was understood to be only an initial exercise in a more long-term funding operation. Nor is it difficult to appreciate the attraction that a strong and well-equipped National Front might have for right-wing, and cynical, Conservative dissidents who are prepared to expend considerable effort and resource in pressuring their party into hard-line political rightism. Indeed, as shall be illustrated later, ulterior motives of all kinds and from quite surprising quarters play a significant role in the funding of extreme parties.

The National Front has for some time been operating a number of limited companies of its own. Among them are to be found NF Properties Limited, Leachouse Limited, Benjuya Limited and NF Information Services Limited through which the Front has sought to legitimise its business operations. Excalibur House for instance, the

Party's former HQ in Shoreditch's Great Eastern Street, is owned by NF Properties and leased to Leachouse, a 'storage and warehousing' group. Hackney Council however, was by no means convinced that the property was not being used as political offices, a usage which contravenes planning regulations. The legal battle arising out of this conflict of 'interpretations' has itself become a political *cause célèbre*, well documented in the national press.

The National Front indeed, has met with a considerable series of reverses over 73, Great Eastern Street, EC2. Hackney Council has barred NF Properties Ltd from using part of the building as a social club; the Council has also denied Leachouse Ltd planning permission to use the ground floor as a printing workshop. Meanwhile the Secretary of State, Michael Heseltine, has confirmed another Council ruling which required the National Front to cease using the building as administrative headquarters and offices.*

Indeed in general the National Front does not make much distinction between its business and political interests. NF Properties, which is the channel for NF funds, has a list of shareholders which makes interesting reading. Among them is Andrew Fountaine, Commander RNR and former Francoist soldier, who was once a member of the Conservative Party and a parliamentary candidate, ex vice-chairman of the National Front and wealthy Norfolk landowner; another ex-Tory shareholder is Squadron Leader John Harrison-Broadley, an executive with a car-hire firm. Yet another shareholder with a military background and former Unionist parliamentary candidate for the Orkneys is Lt. Commander Michael C.F. Forsyth-Grant, a wealthy Scottish landowner and director of a salmon-fisheries farm, who according to the Front itself is 'a very good financial supporter'. Forsyth-Grant, while falsely claiming that he is not an NF member, once told the Glasgow *Sunday Mail*:

> I believe in a strong centre party. That's why I sympathise with the National Front. I call myself a National Socialist. The world's greatest Nationalist was Adolf Hitler. Fascism is greatly misunderstood in this country.

Another shareholder of less blameless a military career is Dr W. John Mitchell, who was court-martialled during World War 2 for his explicitly pro-German sympathies; his son Dr R.G. Mitchell is also a shareholder. Building company director George Wright is also on the list, as are, among others, Barbara Elizabeth Webb, James

---

* Since this final ruling the National Front have vacated the premises.

Wells, Trevor Malcolm Smith, J. Parfett and Desmond Fenwick. The company's directors include Paul Kavanagh of Kavanagh, O'Moore and Co. Ltd., Michael Stubbs and Donald Bruce, Douglas David Priest is Company Secretary.

The prominence of Fountaine and Kavanagh is especially interesting, and indeed currently highly embarrassing to the National Front itself for they have been prime movers in the breakaway Constitutional Movement's campaign to unseat Tyndall and Webster from their eminent party offices. The NF splinter, the British Democratic Party (formerly known as the British People's Party) which recently left the Front took with it not only the properties in Nottingham and Leicester which it occupies, but also the Front's membership lists and subscriptions. Even more crucially, the dissident group controls NF Properties and thus Excalibur House. The National Front has therefore at a blow lost its properties and its subscriptions. Not surprisingly the Front has opened court proceedings against the renegades of the British Democratic Party which is led by Anthony Reed Herbert, the Front's solicitor in the Hackney Council hearings. So reduced are the circumstances of the rump of the Front, that, as the *News of the World* reported (3 August 1980), Excalibur House 'has become a warehouse for hard-core pornography.' A spokesman for the Front, told the interviewer:

> Going into the dirty books business is the only way the party can survive with dwindling funds and the possibility of bankruptcy proceedings.

One of the especially interesting features in the case of the acquisition of Excalibur House is that the National Front launched an appeal among its membership for a total of £76,000 for the purchase of premises. Research shows that the party actually bought premises in Nottingham and Leicester for a total of £35,000 and that £44,000 was paid for the acquisition of Excalibur House, making a grand total of £79,000. But, as illustrated, a private limited company was formed with 28 named shareholders, specifically to put up the money for Headquarters and which consequently owns the building. What then, has become of the £76,000, or for what purpose has it been deployed?

Thought-provoking as they may be, these connections and finance methods by no means account for the full extent of right-wing extremist funding networks. The following evidence serves as an example of other more disturbing channels. On 28 January 1976,

Mr V.J. Lewis replied on official headed notepaper to an enquiry from the British Movement. Mr Lewis was at that time Acting Director of Information for the Smith regime in Rhodesia:

> I refer to your letter addressed to the Principal Private Secretary to the Prime Minister ... I regret the delay in replying which has been occasioned by efforts on our part to examine the feasibility of your proposal.
>
> I very much regret that we are unable to offer financial assistance due to the many difficulties we have in transfering (sic) foreign currency. However, if we can assist in any other way, for example, by providing photographic or written material for your publication, *The Patriot*, then please do not hesitate to let me know.

The Rhodesian Government was clearly not ill-disposed to the Movement or its proposal and it would indeed be interesting to know how many other foreign sources the group attempted to tap and with what success.

For obvious reasons governments are not as a rule prepared to fund directly those foreign, or domestic, groups which they consider either worthy or useful. But there are many means by which a government may benefit an organisation of its choice. The governments of Taiwan, South Korea and Saudi Arabia for instance, subsidise to a very considerable degree the World Anti-Communist League; and WACL itself inevitably channels funds into its various national affiliated bodies, including the British League of Rights.

Many governments, including notably those of Libya, Iraq and Saudi Arabia, employ similar means by which to fund extremist groups which they consider useful in their international anti-Zionist campaigns. Such operations, which are particularly intently focused on the UK, France and West Germany, are usually conducted through Public Relations enterprises and often through an intermediary, namely the PLO. Indeed the Libyan government has placed at least $30m in Swiss bank accounts at the disposal of the PLO for its propaganda promotional purposes. Libya itself spends approximately £1m in Britain alone in its anti-Zionist campaign, and much of that money finds its way to extremist groups of one complexion or another. Specifically, the Libyans have financed the printing and publication of 500,000 copies of the infamously anti-Semitic booklet *Did Six Million Really Die?* which were then 'exported' from Britain for distribution abroad, principally in the USA. Recent allegations indicate that Libyan involvements extend beyond the financial and propaganda interests: both in the USA and in the UK it has been reported that Libyan diplomats have been abusing their immunity by importing arms and ammunition in their luggage. The Saudi Arabians have also engaged in activities with similarly offensive literature. Saudi legations and Embassies throughout the world have been promoting and distributing the notorious *Protocols of the Elders of Zion.* Indeed Libya, Saudi Arabia and Iraq actually commission a British Public Relations firm allegedly to stimulate anti-Zionist and anti-Semitic material among writers and journalists.

Beyond a doubt, the extreme right in Britain has acquired funds, and therefore long-term and broadly-based operational capacities, quite out of proportion to their actual strength in membership and immediate domestic importance. The various groups have established international networks of affiliations and alliances which greatly increase the potential threat that they offer. Increasingly substantial amounts of money flow from larger and wealthier fascist and nazi groups in the United States, West Germany, France and Spain as well as from foreign governments and agencies and these sums are filtered from one British organisation to another. For such 'investment', patrons naturally expect some substantial return; there is no reason to suppose that to date they have been dissatisfied.

Finance: the Militant Tendency and the Left

The funding of left-wing extremists is no less covert and intriguing than that of the right. Indeed, many of the procedures involved are identical; more strikingly, some of the benefactors and patrons, as shall be shown, are the very same.

The recent press and media stampede to expose the Militant Tendency's infiltration into the Labour Party first gathered momentum when, on 16 December 1979, the *Sunday Times* ran an article entitled, 'Who gave £148,500 to Trots?' Since that initial speculation, several subsidiary questions have been put and enquiries made; to date however, no conclusive answers have been forthcoming. The importance and relevance of that headline should not however be underestimated. The arguments which rage over what in theory constitutes infringement or subversion of Labour Party regulations will doubtless continue towards no conclusion –

other than, by default, a vindication of the Tendency's tactics. But, if substantive evidence can be presented which proves that the Militant Tendency is in receipt, by whatever means, of monies for political activities distinct from Labour Party activities and beyond the legitimate projects of the *Militant* newspaper and its editorial staff, then allegations and suspicions that the Tendency is in fact a party apparatus within another party, will be indisputably confirmed.

The £148,500 to which the *Sunday Times* refers is a loan disclosed in the annual reports of Cambridge Heath Press, which publishes *Militant*. The loan is vital to Militant, as the *Sunday Times* points out:

> ... without the injection of these funds from an unidentified source, the group would not have been able to operate on anything like its present scale, which seriously alarms many Labour MPs.

Cambridge Heath itself is similarly reliant:

> ... 1978-9 accounts have not yet been filed, but previous returns show loan instalments received of £50,000 in 1975, £48,500 in 1976 and £50,000 in 1977. Without them Cambridge Heath would not have continued as a going concern. Accumulated losses for the years 1975-8 amounted to £145,000.

These sums appear not to have emanated either from institutional funds or from banks, since neither outstanding charges against Cambridge Heath nor substantial interest rates figure in the accounts.

As is to be expected, the relationship between the *Militant* and Cambridge Heath Press is an intimate one: Peter Taaffe, editor of *Militant*, is a director of Cambridge Heath. In turn, Cambridge Heath has a close relationship with, or perhaps resemblance to, another company, Workers International Review Publications which was set up in its present form in 1973. Taaffe's editorial colleague and Militant 'guru' Ted Grant, is a director of WIR Publications. Indeed, according to the *New Statesman* (18 January 1980), the 25 WIR shareholders are all Militant supporters, a large number of whom have served on the editorial board:

> WIR received a series of donations from 1974 to 1978, rising from £18,000 to £77,000 in the last year. Much of this money, amounting to some £236,000, was transferred to Cambridge Heath and probably constituted the levy on members' salaries. The loans given by WIR exactly match the loans received by Cambridge Heath.

Not only do the size of the loans coincide, but so also do the period of those loans, their repayment date and their interest date. The evidence may be circumstantial; nevertheless it is compelling. Moreover, Cambridge Heath's auditors, Norton Shaw and Nathan, value the company as a 'going concern' since they assume, as they correctly estimated in their 1976 report, that 'the company will continue to receive the financial support it is receiving at present.' That is to say, that Cambridge Heath is dependent upon WIR, without the financial aid of which it would face bankruptcy. The Labour lawyer Charles James, having spent three years researching this case, has no doubts as to these crucial relationships. Given its considerable trading losses, James believes, Militant would have undoubtedly have been declared bankrupt by the auditors but for the timely securing of these substantial loans.

It should not be forgotten that the Militant Tendency is a large-scale operation. It employs 63 full-time workers – a large number for the purposes of a weekly political newspaper – half of whom are based at headquarters in Mentmore Terrace in the East End of London. Their income is supposedly derived from a tithe on working supporters. A secret internal letter dispatched in 1978 under the imprint of 'C' informed local organisers that 'the average receipt per comrade per week based on the three months to September including the International Levy was £1.17, a drop from £1.22 the average of the previous year.' It is highly unlikely that such an amount, even supplemented by the proceeds of collections at meetings and the usual jumble sale routine, could support the activities of the Militant group. Indeed the Militant newspaper, with a print order of 9,350, has a considerably smaller circulation – though its readership is higher – and is a far from profitable commodity. In fact it loses about £12,000 a year through what the editorial board describes as 'lack of accounting', commonly understood as 'fingers in the till' on the part of its sellers. Clearly, the Militant Tendency is critically dependent upon other sources of income.

But if the Tendency is funded through the newspaper, and if the newspaper is supported by Cambridge Heath Press; and if Cambridge Heath Press depends upon Workers International Review Publications, from what source does WIR Publications derive its surplus income?

Research has revealed that supporters, if they are not to be called 'party members' of the Militant Tendency, do pay subscriptions, not only for the paper, but to the Tendency itself. These monies are paid by bank-debit, through a standing order which transfers the drafts to a holding fund which itself acts as a cover and front for Militant. That 'holding' company may well prove to be none other than WIR Publications. In any event, the members of Militant Tendency, if no-one else, obviously regard themselves as fully paid-up members of one other party besides the Labour Party.

Most of the other extreme left-wing groups are not quite so beset by the logistic and legalistic problems which complicate the Militant Tendency's funding operation. Either their activities and size of full-time staff, except in the case of the Socialist Workers' Party, do not demand so large a budget, or their non-entrist strategy avoids the embargo on certain avenues of finance.

Nevertheless, it is difficult to see how many of these groups which often produce well-presented and voluminous publications on a regular basis could possibly finance their considerable efforts without equally considerable subsidies. The Workers' Revolutionary Party, as has been noted, is the only party left of centre in Britain, excluding the Communist Party but including the Labour Party, which is able to produce a daily paper. *Newsline* is a sixteen-page tabloid with regular colour features which sells at 10p a copy. The chances of so ambitious a project financing itself are slender. But on the other hand, its unremitting idolisation of Colonel Gadaffi and Yasser Arafat hints strongly at two possible sources of subsidy.

The alliances which exist between the parties of the right, be they cordial or covert, do not in normal circumstances occur to the same degree or extent on the left for the sectarian and pious reasons already discussed. The distribution of funds therefore from a common source within the extreme left or from one group to another is not a major factor. Nor are the European parties usually in a position to fund their British counterparts to the degree that occurs on the right. In general therefore, the extreme left has either to find its funds through subscriptions and appeals, or direct from paymasters.

The Socialist Workers' Party undoubtedly benefitted from its sponsorship of the Anti-Nazi League for, while it may not actually have 'creamed off' any of the League's funds, it certainly profitted from the strength and efficiency that the campaign lent to the party. Indeed the ANL's fund-raising effort has been impressive. The *Daily Telegraph* reported on 26 April 1979:

Trouble in the crowd as the Socialist League counter-demonstrates against the National Front in Lewisham.

The latest figures show that in 1978 the Anti-Nazi League's income from private and trade union donations amounted to around £175,000. Donations vary from £250 from a trade union to the £1 postal order from a private citizen.

It is significant however, that defections from the League were frequently a response to the overt political and recruitment campaign that the SWP has been waging. Indeed, although the League itself had originally been financed by a Jewish businessman, as SWP involvement intensified, so Jewish support diminished for, as the *Sunday Telegraph* (5 March 1978), pointed out:

> It is the similarities between the Socialist Workers and the National Front that are so diverting. Not only are there identical points of economic policy, but the 'anti-Zionism' of the two groups is also equally virulent.

In view of this common feature, it is not so surprising to find that the governments of Libya, Iraq and Saudi Arabia take as much interest in the activities of the extreme left as they do of the extreme right. Once again the PLO acts both for itself and for these, and other Arab nations in the liaison with and funding of British groups of the extreme left; once again specifically ear-marked funds take a most circuitous route before finally arriving at their destination. Whole continents are not necessarily an obstacle: both Iraq and the Soviet Union fund the obscenely anti-Semitic US Labor Party which in turn supports the European Workers' Party which itself disburses funds to various sympathetic factions.

Unsurprisingly, the USSR itself plays its role in the support of far-left groups, even when, as with the Trotskyists, they are completely and mutually and implaccably inimical. A standard method employed in such funding techniques involves the transferral of funds from East Germany to extremist groups in West Germany. Thence they are distributed throughout the Continent, often with the ultimate beneficiary entirely unaware of the source of his donation and without the vaguest notion as to the identity of his patron. Thus it occurs that extremist groups themselves can frequently become the unconscious dupes of somewhat more powerful interests and somewhat less sympathetic motives.

The funding issue is a far-reaching issue. In the wake of disclosures that a number of American Congressmen face prosecution over alleged acceptance of Arab bribes, allegations have also been made that British politicians have been induced, albeit in all probable innocence if ill-advisedly, to accept contributions towards their respective party's funds. Militant also, while fending off threats of official Labour Party investigation, came up with a scoop of its own, proclaiming across the centre spread of its newspaper, (1 February 1980), 'How the CIA Funded Labour's Right Wing'. A month later the *Times* of 5 March headlined the news that 'Nato gave £32,335 to Labour moderates'.

Replying in writing to an enquiry from Lord Brockway, Lord Carrington stated that since 1976, Nato had provided a total of £32,335 to a Labour Party/TUC press service known as the Labour Committee for Transatlantic Understanding. Its sponsors, under the chairmanship of Roy Mason, include Roy Hattersley, Dr David Owen and William Rodgers – all prominent members on the right of the Labour Party – and from the trade unions, Frank Chapple, Terry Duffy, Bill Sirs and Sid Weighell. As reputable as these figures may be, Lord Brockway asserted (*Times*, 5 March 1980):

> I regard it as reprehensible that Nato should be funding a section within a political party, a section which has been campaigning against its national executive and the left wing. But I would be just as against money coming from external sources to the left wing.

In mid-February the Labour Party pledged itself to investigate all the allegations of entrism and untoward funding. When the organisation sub-committee of the party's national executive voted to instigate investigations into Militant Tendency and other Trotskyist groups associated with the Labour Party, the Young Socialist representative, Tony Saunois of Militant, proposed an amendment, which was accepted, which committed any enquiry to include an examination of the roles played in Party affairs by the CIA and by businessmen and industrialists. By the end of the month the decision had been reversed when the NEC announced, no doubt to the mutual relief of both right and left members, that it was 'not its wish to set up an inquisition into the activities of groups within the party.' Instead, it invited all known inner-party groups, under no compulsion, to publish details of their aims, organisation, finance and membership. *Labour Weekly* reported (29 February 1980):

> If they don't it will be up to party members to draw their own conclusions, said general secretary Ron Hayward.

As is quite apparent the investigation of party finance is as problematic as it is revealing. Particularly in the extremist hinterland, funding strategies are as complex and devious as the politics and activities they promote. But there is a further element which proceeds from the alliances, involvements and loyalties which ideology, strategy and indebtedness combine to produce on the international scene: terrorism.

Internationalism and Alliance: Terrorism

It has been a natural and indeed inevitable development in world politics that as economic and military alliances and strategies expand and proliferate across national and continental frontiers, so in parallel do those movements which seek to subvert or destroy them. Similarly the age of technological achievement has benefitted the observant citizen and the cynical revolutionary alike. The latter, with all the advantages and opportunities of modern, sophisticated communications systems, transport and weaponry at his disposal and with the benefit of logistic support on an international scale and the promise of 'safe havens' worldwide, can pinpoint his target and execute his project with alarming facility and to maximum effect. Kidnapping, hijacking, the seizure of hostages, bomb-attacks and assassinations have become so regular a feature of political and commercial life that they hardly command front-page coverage in the world's press. In only fifteen years, international terrorism has established itself as a form of alternative politic which, in importance, transcends the purely criminal. In the next decade the terrorist international will have achieved the status of a kind of satanic United Nations. At a seminar on terrorism held in Chicago in November 1979, the expert Dr Yonah Alexander, editor of the journal *Terrorism*, was reported in the *Times* as having forecast that 'terrorists would get their hands on nuclear weapons in 5 to 10 years. Today they can acquire anti-tank rockets which can be fired at nuclear installations.'

Terrorism in Britain does not have a strong tradition; the activities of the Angry Brigade of the early 1970s were as sporadic and ill-conceived as they were short-lived; the attacks perpetrated by the IRA, and the extravagant vandalism practiced occasionally by the Scottish and Welsh Nationalists, have been more nationalistic than political in inspiration. The letter- and fire-bombings and the desecrations carried out by the extreme right have been poorly concerted and spasmodic and in general more of a

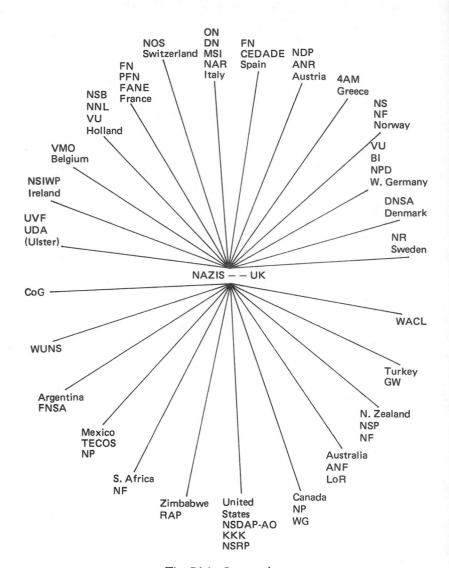

The Right Connections

Key to the Right Connections

Argentina: FNSA – Argentinian National Socialist Front
Australia: ANF – Australian National Front/LoR – League of Rights
Austria: ANR – New Right Action/NDP – National Democratic Party
Belgium: VMO – Flemish Militant Order
Canada: NP – National Party/WG – Western Guard
Denmark: DNSA – Danish National Socialist Alliance
France: FANE – Federation of National and European Action/PFN – New Force Party/FN – National Front
W. Germany: NPD – National Democratic Party/BI – 'Burger-initiative'/VU – Folkish Union
Greece: 4AM – 4th August Movement
Holland: VU – Folkish Union/NNL – Nazi Northern League/NSB – Nat. Soc. Movement
Ireland: NSIWP – National Socialist Irish Workers' Party
Italy: MSI – Italian Socialist Movement/DN – National Right/ON – New Order/NAR – Revolutionary Armed Nuclei
Mexico: 'TECOS'/NP – Nazi Party
New Zealand: NSP – National Socialist Party/NF – National Front
Norway: NF – Norsk Front/NS – 'Natjional Samling'
South Africa: NF – National Front
Spain: 'CEDADE'/FN – New Force
Sweden: NR – 'Nordiska Rikspartiet'
Switzerland: NOS – New Social Order
Turkey: GW – 'Grey Wolves'
U.S.A. : NSDAP-AO – American Nazi Party/KKK – Ku Klux Klan/NSRP – National States Rights Party
Zimbabwe: RAP – Rhodesia Action Party
CoG: Children of God
W.A.C.L. : World Anti-Communist League
W.U.N.S. : World Union of National Socialists
(Ulster: UDA – Ulster Defence Association/UVF – Ulster Volunteer Force)

criminal than a terroristic nature. On the part of the extreme left, the relative success of its recent, particularly entrist, strategies, has largely precluded any serious employment of terrorist tactics.

Nonetheless, it should be recognised that the organisation exists and that the contacts are established through which terrorist activity in Britain can at any time be countenanced. Terrorist outrages prosecuted on the British mainland by the IRA emphasise this point. Allegations that the IRA and PLO shared an occasionally intimate relationship have long been rife. They have for almost as long been denied. However, during the course of the trial of Brian Keenan, IRA Quarter-Master General who directed the bombing campaign of 1975 which killed nine and injured 100 Londoners, substantial evidence was produced which firmly linked the two terrorist groups. Keenan himself, who had learned Arabic, not only visited the PLO, but also, amongst others, the Baader-Meinhof group. Libya also received Keenan in the course of his search for arms supplies. When Keenan was arrested in Belfast in March 1979, he had in his possession a coded diary containing the phone numbers of terrorist groups and other potential gun-running groups throughout the world, in the Middle East, Europe, Japan, the USA. The evidence strongly suggested that Keenan, convicted and sentenced to 18 years imprisonment, had links, as the *Guardian* put it, 'with virtually every terrorist group in the world.'

It is certainly the case, as has been documented in preceding sections of this paper, that compact highly-trained and well-equipped commando units, such as Wotan and Column 88, exist on the extreme right. It is known that such outfits have considerable foreign connections and that they see themselves as supra-national 'political soldiers'. I have recently acquired material circulated to British extremist groups of the right which emanates from the French 'Federation d'Action Nationale et Europeenne', inviting 'foreign comrades' to a muster camp in the 'wildest quarter of the Central Pyrenees' where the uniformed cadres of all European extreme right groups engaged in August 1979 in diverse activities, 'covering the classics of our ideology, rhetoric and propaganda, self-defence and guerilla techniques'. FANE itself has since been suppressed by the French Government (3 September 1980). But the organisations which it has spawned, and which operate from FANE's former address in Paris, are pursuing identical objectives. Following hard on the heels of the atrocious bomb attack on Bologna railway station, apparently perpetrated by the

Revolutionary Armed Nuclei (NAR), came the bomb blast in a Munich beer-hall and the bomb attack on a Paris synagogue. Responsibility for the Paris outrage has been claimed by the National European Fasces (FNE) which is largely the reborn FANE. It will not be surprising to note that FANE's relationship with NAR has been intimate – as has been its contact with the League of Saint George in Britain. Links between left and right terrorist groups are slightly more unexpected, but as *Paesa Sera*, the Italian newspaper, put it 'they are branches of the same tree.' There is in fact substantial evidence that the 'red' and 'black' terror groups in Italy have formed alliances: of a cache of stolen weapons, half were discovered in a fascist hide-out, half in a Red Brigade arsenal. The Red Brigades had carried out the theft. It is known also that in 1976 at a 'summit meeting' in Calabria, the leader of the leftist Prima Linea, Corrado Alunni (since arrested) came together with the leader of the NAR Sergio Calore, one of the accused in the Bologna bomb trial.

Such activity needs no commentary. But there is another aspect of international terrorism which is possibly yet more significant and more imminently realisable. For while extremist groups may not be prepared, either conceptually or actually, to conduct acts of terrorism on their own behalf, they may be, indeed have been, (for instance, in the notable case of the Japanese Red Army in the Lod massacre) induced to accept commissions from other less circumspect quarters – to put it at its crudest: money talks.

A serious explosion of urban terrorism in any country in Europe, not excluding Britain, is a certain possibility. There exists a concerted network in the terrorist community which ensures at all times the availability of logistic support, of personnel, of weaponry and communications, of training, of funding, of information and intelligence services and of expertise. In this country, the proven links which exist for instance between the extreme left and the IRA, and the extreme right and Ulster Protestant para-military groups illustrate only the tip of the iceberg. Even in Italy, where terrorism has become a permanent feature of social life, it is believed that active guerillas are to be counted in tens rather than hundreds; but as the *Times* (23 January 1980), reported, they 'are highly trained and professional, which cannot always be said of the police.' So the question is crucial: who sponsors the terrorists? As the Italian

President Signor Pertini asked (*Times*, 2 January 1980):

> Is it perhaps pure coincidence that until now not one weapon of Italian manufacture has been found in terrorist lairs, but all are of foreign make? Who in the shadows is conspiring against our democracy?

It is indeed becoming ever more clear that at least one foreign nation with a sizable investment in Italian terrorism is Libya. According to Italian security officials, it is alleged that Colonel Gadaffi has provided almost £1m to Sardinian separatist groups, was involved in the brutal kidnap and murder of Christian Democrat leader Aldo Moro and, latterly, in the massacre at Bologna railway station in August 1980. The Italian Interior Ministry is currently investigating evidence that Gadaffi not only has a terrorist support-group inside Italy, but also is providing training facilities for as many as 5000 Italian terrorists of both extreme right and left in Libya, at Zuara, Gadames, Simauen, Oufra, El-Beida, Tobruk and Joud al Daim.

Nor by any means are such operations limited to Italy. As Robert Moss reported (*Daily Telegraph*, 4 August 1980), Colonel Gadaffi's Information Minister Muhammad al-Zuwway has publicly proclaimed:

> We assert to the whole world that we provide material, moral and political support to every liberation revolution in the world.

The spider in the centre of the terrorist web is, beyond a doubt, the Palestine Liberation Organisation. The PLO, with huge financial and indeed diplomatic resources at their disposal, have a world-wide operation which is both legitimate and considerably less so. The PLO has established contacts with an extremely comprehensive roll-call of far left and right groups throughout the world: the Japanese Red Army, the Tupamaros of Uruguay, Frolinad of Chad, the West German Baader-Meinhof and Red Army Fraction and Nazi groups – the Palestine Liberation Army (PLA) recently advertised in the *Deutsche National-Zeitung* for the 'assistance' of young neo-nazis in the Palestinian 'liberation struggle' – with the Italian Red Brigades, with French Nazi groups and with the Organisation of the Children of God, which recently initiated an understanding with the League of St George, with the IRA and with several other groups including the British League of Rights and the Socialist Workers' Party in Britain, with the Cedade in Spain, with both the Ku Klux Klan and the Black Panthers in the USA, with the Basque underground and with groups in Eritrea, Puerto Rico, Turkey and

Morocco; the list is endless. The PLO funds, supports and trains a large proportion of these groups without particular attention to their political aims or ideological commitment. The 'two-track' approach to which it has been suggested the National Front is turning in Britain, has masterfully been exemplified by the PLO throughout the world. As Robert Moss pointed out in the *Daily Telegraph* (3 December 1979), the PLO has developed a strategy which enables it to give 'public pledges of moderation while continuing to work secretly with the (Baader-Meinhof) underground.' Token of the profit to the PLO at least, of such a strategy, is the somewhat alarming blandness of British Foreign Secretary, Lord Carrington, when he recognised in a speech of 17 March 1980, merely 'some elements of the PLO which in the past have been associated with terrorists' and concluded that he did not think that 'the PLO, as such, is a terrorist organisation.' This is not simply an unguarded or personal opinion. In reply to a written enquiry, a senior Foreign Office Civil Servant stated a month later:

> In our view it is an over-simplification to describe the PLO as a terrorist organisation. It is rather a political umbrella movement, though one which ... includes within it groups which continue to be involved with terrorist activities.'

In essence the 'two-track' strategy is extremely simple; while the PLO strives energetically to build upon its reputation as a political and diplomatic mission, it deputes its less 'moderate', and consequently more embarrassing activities to other extremist groups on its payroll. The fact that the PLO clients themselves have no more in common with each other besides their extremism only serves to emphasise the point that terrorism has become a kind of multi-national industry devoid entirely of any ideological idealism or piety — a factor which makes it all the more difficult to predict or anticipate.

The direct consequences are threefold: firstly, the PLO achieves its terrorist ends, and without undue publicity; secondly, extremist groups gain otherwise unexpected funds, experience, weaponry and contacts; thirdly, those influences which guide the PLO fulfill their own objectives.

For not even the PLO is prime-mover in the terrorist international. Without the financial subsidy of Syria, Libya, Iraq and Saudi Arabia, without the support of Cuba, Algeria and Vietnam, and most significantly in this context, without the tutelage and patronage of the Soviet Union, the PLO itself would be no more than a small and savage band of guerillas.

In the terrorist chain, every agent benefits according to his immediate or far-distant ambitions, however unconnected or inimical they may superficially appear to be. In his paper 'The PLO and the USSR' (September 1979), Robert Moss provides an appropriately typical example of the profitable convolutions of the process from the general to the particular terrorist objectives; the process is known in US Intelligence as the Soviets' 'low intensity warfare' strategy:

> ... Soviet-made Strela missiles came to be in the hands of Joshua Nkomo's guerilla movement, which used them to shoot down two civilian airliners from its bases in Zambia. Western analysts believe that what happened in that instance was a rather complicated transaction. The Russians supplied Strelas to Libya, which in turn passed some of them on to the PLO, which in turn played the part of benefactor to Nkomo's forces.

As with certain funding operations already discussed, the donor and the recipient have separate and distinct interests in a single transaction. The most unlikely alliances are made. But the Soviets and their proxies will not scruple to support covertly even the most unsympathetic or antagonistic groups if they prove sufficiently embarrassing or threatening to Western governments; similarly, such groups will not scruple to accept support for their own quite obvious reasons; often the source of that aid is by no means the primary source. The strategy is two-fold; firstly and quite obviously, it protects both the donor and the recipient; secondly, and most importantly, it also enables the paymaster surreptitiously to infiltrate an extremist organisation and to insinuate his influence in its operation.

Overt contact between foreign governments and extremist groups is not an infrequent occurrence; Libya's Colonel Gadaffi has on occasion met leaders of both extreme left and extreme right British groups in the furtherance of the Arab anti-Zionist campaign. More covert activity is periodically uncovered; at the end of January 1980 the Soviet Ambassador to New Zealand was expelled from that country after the government had discovered his involvement with and funding of the far left Socialist Unity Party. Clearly the more covert and undetected machinations, such as those alluded to above, are by definition normally undetectable.

But sources have revealed a quite remarkable and far-reaching development in the case of the Militant Tendency. Towards the end of January 1980, as the controversy over Militant's presence within the Labour Party gathered momentum, the Soviet KGB dispatched from Paris to this country one of its top specialist agents briefed to infiltrate the Tendency itself with the object so far as possible of shielding it from complete or damaging exposure. When it is considered that the Soviets have anathematised Trotsky and all his works to the extent of removing his image from official and historical photographs, and that most Trotskyists similarly despise the Kremlin, such a move seems especially confounding, not to mention implausible. But it is nevertheless a very sound strategy, given Militant's embarrassment to and influence in the Labour Party. Ultimately, it may well be that the Militants are as efficiently duped and entered as had the Labour Party been by the Tendency itself. It should also be recognised that currently, when the Militant Tendency is infiltrated, so simultaneously and implicitly, is the Labour Party.

It is clear then, that even if extreme groups do not of themselves engage in terrorist campaigns, there is no assurance that they will, may or do not lend local and logistical support to international guerilla groups. It is clear also that foreign governments have taken, do take and will take considerable interest in the facilities which extremist groups have to offer, either in terms of personnel, intelligence and logistic resources or through their own direct activities. It should be remembered also that the groups themselves are vulnerable to the 'interventionism' of more powerful interests.

With recent developments in Iran and yet more crucially in Afghanistan, the world appears to have slipped dangerously towards the Cold War syndrome. This situation, and the potential explosivity of the Middle East arena mean that those foreign governments already involved in international subversion – and Gadaffi's Libya is a case in point – will intensify their operations.

The existence in Britain of extremist groups of either right or left is in itself regrettable. But in the international context, the presence of those groups which, for political or tactical motives of their own or for those of others, are equipped to operate their strategies effectively and subversively, renders them at the very least a national liability, and at worst a committed and efficient Fifth Column.

Solutions and Counter Strategies

The principal point of this paper has been to advertise the extent of the problem which political extremism poses for a democracy such as Britain's. To the extent that this report will be read and found informative, it will have partially succeeded in that declared aim and, albeit to a limited degree, it will have offered a solution to the problem it addresses. For in a democratic and liberal society ignorance and its companion complacency can constitute a more substantial threat to the health of the body of the nation than can the tiny hostile viruses which periodically attack its constitution. It is to be hoped that material information has been presented and cogent arguments have been persuasively advanced which counsel against such critical and self-hazardous complacency. As has been suggested earlier, democratic freedoms are not facts per se, they are guiding principles designed to inspire and direct social and political conduct not to stupify or inhibit it. Freedom's abstract and intellectual propositions are not merely the subjects for liberal meditation, and the faithful assertion and repetition that one or other freedom is 'inalienable' or 'self-evident' offers neither protection to its obvious and inherent vulnerabilities, nor service to its cause.

Precedents for the jeopardy in which moral and political complacency places a free and democratic society are close to hand. The stricture of an early British Ambassador to Washington, Admiral Bryce, that the American constitution was perilously 'all sail and no anchor' was well, if belatedly, remembered at the height of the reverberating Watergate disaster. The notional strength of freedoms elusively though speedily and surely evaporates unless it be resolutely, continuously and actively embodied.

The first principle towards an understanding and resolution of the problems discussed therefore, must be vigilance; the second is the resolve and will to act. If an institution is worth saving, it must actively be preserved.

Information

The first problem to be encountered is that of information. Public awareness of extremist activities is often limited to its more theatrical features; not much more is known of the Workers' Revolutionary Party than that its membership can boast the example of an international filmstar. The antics of extreme groups may appear ridiculous, but they are not.

Information is obviously crucially important. Extremist groups do not often seek publicity and limit their self-advertisement to carefully plotted and analysed adventures. It is indeed remarkable that in the necessary research for this paper, the author was not able to call upon a single comprehensive source or survey of the current political fringe. The paper that is offered here breaks new ground in this respect, but it is in itself insubstantial. The surface has been no more than scratched: there is much digging to be done.

But it must be emphasised that it should not be the responsibility of private individuals to take up the burden of exposing to the nation's public and indeed to the political institutions themselves, the dangers and subversions that are energetically undermining their social fabric. Nor is it necessarily advisable or appropriate that private interests are left, from their own motives, to render such politically charged accounts.

Concerted efforts are imperative on two fronts. First, those of position and authority must acquaint themselves with the threat presented by political extremism in its broadest aspects and within the scope of its ramifications and indeed, implications. An overview is essential.

Second, those who constitute the recruiting target of the extremists must be induced to understand the broadest aims of the activists and the strategies by which they themselves can be so easily and involuntarily manipulated. The 'grass roots' awareness of political motive and operation is essential.

Certain of the campaigns led by the extremists of left and right are more or less easily identified. Others are more subtle: the infiltration of the trade unions and the constituency parties by discreet and ingenious activists is a problem which has not seriously been tackled, partly through lack of leadership and resolve at the top, partly because of the apathy of those more directly involved. In either sector, the extent and consequences of entrist militancy and its motivation have not been properly understood. In all these contexts, this paper is no more than indicative. Still more searching, exhaustive and comprehensive enquiries remain to be undertaken, and published. There are many and serious questions to be asked of the extreme groups, their agents and patrons before the liberal concept of 'broad church' democracy can be confidently vindicated.

Action

As stated above, the remedy against extremist threats to democracy is to be found in resolve and responsibility, and not in legislation. Democracy cannot be administered by statute and decree. When it becomes inevitably necessary for the full force of government to be applied against extremist incursions, it will already, and coincidentally, be too late.

The responsibility falls necessarily upon the individual citizen to appreciate, respect and protect his freedoms. That responsibility falls yet more onerously upon the representatives and promoters of those freedoms. It is absurd that successive Labour and Conservative governments should appoint themselves to preach moderation and amity to their electors in the interests of the national welfare, while they themselves at all party levels harbour unchastised or undetected, the very seeds of disruption and division.

The major parties in particular must look to their own constitutional democracy and must be able to satisfy and assure the electorate that they are preserving both their integrity and their popular mandate. This implies neither 'witch-hunt' nor inquisition; the proscribed list is an established though apparently defunct facility of party politics – the Labour Party's 'list' fell into disuse in 1973.

Similarly, party officials and especially candidates should be obliged to declare their political affiliations and, before appointment or adoption, required to satisfy certain criteria binding on all parties on such critical and basic issues as human rights, civil liberties, national interests etc. There is nothing radical in these suggestions: MPs are already required to divulge, in certain circumstances, commercial interests, defer to the party whip, observe the party constitution and the parliamentary protocol.

In summation, I would suggest the following preliminary measures be taken:

1. That the Government should institute comprehensive research into the full nature of political extremism in Britain, publish its findings and act upon those findings.

2. That the democratic institutions which constitute the social structure of this country — the political parties, the trade unions, the Churches, the educational facilities — be made aware of the threat to their own integrity and be encouraged to take initiatives against that threat, in accordance with democratic principle and in the interests of that principle.

3. That formal procedures be developed by which the institutions are equipped to monitor the activity of pressure groups and respond fittingly to them.

4. That the electorate of Britain is acquainted with the activities and aspirations of extremist political activists.

5. That Government should take counsel with leadership abroad on initiatives against international subversion and terrorism.

The 'cancer in the body politic' has been an almost traditional, indeed perhaps paradoxically vital, component of British democratic life. But its germ must be contained; secondary infection is often fatal.

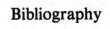

Bibliography

Bibliography

The compilation of a bibliography for a work such as this is not a straightforward project. As has been pointed out, there are no sources of current relevance which provide a comprehensive, or even a broad survey of the periphery of the contemporary political scene in Britain. This volume has depended largely upon original research, upon unpublished papers and upon selective reading. Newspaper articles and study papers, quoted in the text of this book, have also been a principal source of material.

Various institutes publish studies which bear upon the substance of this volume; among them the Institute of Race Relations on the left of centre, and the Institute for the Study of Conflict on the right.

By far the most important source of information on political extremism in Britain is the monthly magazine *Searchlight*, published in Birmingham. *Searchlight* however, concentrates almost exclusively on the activities of the far right. It has no counterpart in scrutinising the left. Nonetheless *Searchlight* should be required reading for any individual who wishes to gain insight into the unsavoury though real world of the political extremists.

With these qualifications in mind, the following bibliography, while not attempting to be comprehensive, provides a useful reading list for those interested in political extremism in contemporary Britain. However, those who would wish to scrutinise the ideologies of the various groups and parties in more precise detail, would do well to study their numerous newspapers, magazines, journals and tracts, most of which are detailed in the body of the text of this book.

GENERAL

Beer, S.H., *Modern British Politics* (London 1965)
Benewick, R., *Political Violence and Public Order* (London 1969)
Blondel, J., *Political Parties: A Genuine Case for Discontent* (London 1978)

Butler, D., and Stokes, D., *Political Change in Britain* (Harmondsworth 1963)

Drucker, H.M. (ed.), *Multi-Party Britain* (London 1979)

Rose, R., *The Problem of Party Government* (Harmondsworth 1976)

Thayer, G., *The British Political Fringe* (London 1965)

THE RIGHT

Billig, M., *Fascists – A Social Psychological View of the National Front* (London 1978)

Boca, Del A., and Giovana, M., *Fascism Today: A World Survey* (London 1970)

Dummet, A., *A Portrait of English Racism* (Harmondsworth 1973)

Duverger, M., *Party Politics and Pressure Groups* (London 1972)

Edgar, D., Racism, Fascism and the Politics of the National Front (*Race & Class*. 1977)

King, R., and Nugent, N., (eds.), *The British Right* (London 1977)

Lunn, K., and Thurlow, R.C., (eds.), *British Fascism* (London 1980)

Miles, R., and Phizacklea, A., (eds.), *Racism and Political Action in Britain* (London 1979)

Rogger, H., and Weber, E., *The European Right* (London 1965)

Walker, M., *The National Front* (Glasgow 1977)

THE LEFT

McCormick, P., *Enemies of Democracy* (London 1979)

Widgery, D., *The Left in Britain 1956–68* (Harmondsworth 1976)

Index